MW01165116

# 10 TAKES

## *Pacific Northwest Writers*

---

### Perspectives on writing

*Jennifer Roland*

SPRINGFIELD, OREGON

**10 TAKES: Pacific Northwest Writers: *Perspectives on Writing***

Publisher & Founder: *Sharleen Nelson*
Publisher & Founder: *J.V. Bolkan*
Acquisitions Editor: *J.V. Bolkan*
Cover/Book Design & Production: *Sharleen Nelson*
Copy Editor: *Julie Bolkan*

First Edition
ISBN: 978-0-9911931-3-4
Printed in United States of America

GladEye Press
Springfield, Oregon
www.gladeyepress.com

# About GladEye Press

GladEye Press is an independent regional book publisher. Located in Oregon's Willamette valley, we specialize in nonfiction books relating to the Pacific Northwest and the people of the region.

As native Oregonians, we are deeply rooted in the region, and have lived, worked, and played along the coast, in the cities, smaller towns, and many of the places populated by little more than moss, ferns, and trees, or jackrabbits, juniper, and cattle.

We love the northwest. We understand that there are a great many special stories and so much we can all share about this place, and we look forward to being a part of the storytelling.

## About the Author

Jennifer Roland is a freelance and marketing writer with more than 20 years experience in newspaper, magazine, and marketing environments. Jennifer also works as a virtual assistant to writers, helping them build their online presence and connect with readers so they can focus on what they love—writing.

She loves fiction and writes that under the name Jennifer C. Rodland. She hopes to put all of the lessons she learned writing this book into getting more of her fiction works published.

# Acknowledgments

Thank you to my publishers and editors J.V. Bolkan and Sharleen Nelson for believing in me and this book—and, I'm sure, for breathing a sigh of relief when I took my own advice and quit waiting for the muse to visit.

Thank you to CarolLee Kidd, who provided the interview transcriptions for the book.

A huge thank you to my husband and son who put up with all the time I spend in front of the computer instead of spending time with them.

And thanks to you for reading this book. I hope it was as fun for you as it was for me. I'd love to hear your favorite tidbit and which writers you'd like to see me interview next. Email me at jen@10takesonwriting.com and let me know. Also visit 10takesonwriting.com to get downloadable worksheets to help you put the advice in this book into practice.

# Contents

# Introduction

**Writing is my favorite way to learn**
When I confront a new topic or one I need to know more about, I look for a way I can write an article, a paper, or web content about it. So I jumped at the chance to write a book about writing.

The best part of writing is the research. I'm such a research geek. I blame it on the 120-page research project I was required to do for my journalism premajor courses at the University of Oregon. That term, I took the course in which we wrote the paper, and I also took Library 101: Introduction to the Library. I learned so many different ways to find documents in the library and online that friends and colleagues still ask to borrow my Google-fu to find information online.

And the best part of research? The interviews. The worst part of interviews? All the stuff that gets left out of the article.

When you're reading an article or a book chapter, do you ever wonder what else the author and the interview subject talked about? I do. I also wonder what it would be like to get that information without the author's filter—to get an inside look at the conversation. And that's what I wanted to do here. To bring you into the conversations I was having with local writers about their process, what they love about the work, and how they, themselves, have learned and gotten to the point they are at in their career. I used to love watching the TV show "Dinner for Five," where Jon Favreau hosted four Hollywood types who talked about their careers and the industry. That's the feel I wanted to replicate in this book. It's writers sitting around talking about writing. We can get into our processes, the business, the things we've learned and who we've learned them from. You know, all the things our non-writer partners, family members, and friends don't want to hear about. That's not to say that I didn't cut out some of the fluff. The pleasantries ended up on the cutting room floor. As did much of the discussions about our kids, pets, and hobbies. Now, if you'd like to read some of that, email me at jen@10takesonwriting.com. If enough of you want to see some of that stuff, it may end up on the website.

## My philosophy on writing

Writing is writing, whether you are doing nonfiction, essays, poetry, novels, short stories, or any other form you can think of. But each form requires a different mindset, and each highlights different skills. The great thing about these skills, though, is that they build on each other. So if you spend some time paying the bills with freelance writing (what? who does that?), it can help feed your skill in writing fiction. For example, when you are paid to write articles for a specific audience, you learn to get in your ideal reader's head. What does this person already know? What do I need to teach? How should I say it? You also learn to write fast. You've got to keep that hourly rate up—and find time and energy to write your fiction, too.

## Finding the writers to interview

To help us all learn from each other, I wanted to make sure I talked to writers of multiple genres, so I looked for at least one children's book writer, a novelist, a short story writer, a graphic novelist, a poet, a screenwriter, and a playwright. One critical component for me was to make sure I found writers at different stages in their careers. I also wanted to make sure I covered a broad range of locations in the northwest.

I made a list of genres to cover, slotting in writers and their locations. I started with one writer whose workshops I had attended at the Willamette Writers Conference a few years back, Eric Witchey. I grabbed a few other writers who had presented at the conference too. Then I looked at genre-specific writers groups to find people who had entered competitions or won awards. Googled queries such as "children's books oregon" and "poets idaho" to find people who sounded like they would be interested in joining the conversation. And I connected with some folks that Eric Witchey suggested.

I was thrilled to see how my list was shaping up: A poet I had previously interviewed for an article in *The Writer*; a graphic novelist who is a regular presence at the Rose City Comic Con; a Eugene-based mystery writer whose blog I had followed for years; a *New York Times* bestselling paranormal romance writer; a young adult writer who won the Washington State Book Award; the former poet laureate of Boise, Idaho; a Seattle-based writer who has been publishing children's books since 1990; and a screenwriter who has been heavily involved with the Willamette Writers Conference. Some are northwest natives, and some are transplants from all over the country.

Oddly enough, it was hardest to find a playwright. Every Google search I tried showed people who were in the Portland or Seattle areas. I love the big cities as much as the next person, but I really wanted to make sure my writers were diverse, and that we covered a varied geography. There have to be playwrights outside of Portland and Seattle, right? Struck by inspiration, I searched for "playwright bend oregon." I came across Cricket Daniel's website. And once I saw that (a) she was funny and (b) she referenced the TV soap *All My Children* in one of her plays, I knew we'd hit it off.

### What you'll find here

In the rest of this book, you'll get to peek in on the conversations I had with these writers. It was so much fun getting into their heads and learning what they love about writing.

I entered into the process with some set questions I wanted to cover—in particular, what it is about the Northwest that draws so many writers. But, as with any conversation, things veered off into unplanned territory with each writer. Everyone has such different backgrounds and diverse experiences in their writing careers. I hope you enjoy reading the interviews as much as I enjoyed conducting them.

# 1 Mary Andonian

Mary Andonian started with quippy essays for parents' magazines and moved into novel writing. After taking a screenwriting class, she realized that was the platform for her. Her current spec script is a thriller called *The Sound of Rain.*

Mary is the film coordinator and former board member for Willamette Writers, one of the largest writing associations in the country. She is the author of the teen inspirational book, *Bitsy's Labyrinth*, which she later adapted into a screenplay. She writes articles and teaches workshops on how to make the most of your writers' conference experience as well as blogs about the writing life. Mary's just starting to dabble in the brave new world of webisode writing.

---

*One of the things I thought was pretty interesting is that you used to write novels and you switched to screenplays. And I'm wondering what it is about screenplays that drew you in and that you love?*

**Mary Andonian:** I do love novel writing. I worked on that novel, *Bitsy's Labyrinth*, for a long time. And before that, I wrote a memoir called *Mind Chatter: Stories from the Squirrel Cage.* What I found out about my writing is I write with brevity. I don't like long soliloquies. I don't like to do super-long descriptions of how the tree looks outside. I like to say "tree."

When I was looking to make the transition from novel writing to screenwriting, I took Cynthia Whitcomb's screenwriting class because one of the holes I had identified in my writing was story structure. Cynthia was the president of Willamette Writers for a long time, and she's an Emmy-winning screenwriter. Screenwriting will help you learn story structure, whether you're writing a novel or a screenplay or a teleplay or a live play. So I wanted to understand that. And I was reading screenwriting books because of that to learn structure and how to tell a story in a structured way, three-act or eight sequences. However you want to do it. And I just loved it. I realized that was what was for me because I can write screenplays the way I write.

My novels come in short because I just don't put in the kind of detail that people really like to read. Yet for screenwriting, you have to be as brief as possible. You have to have as much white space as you can because you have to keep the reader engaged. And then you also have to keep the viewing audience engaged. You can't weight it down with words. So that's why I moved into it. It's a much harder field. Quite Frankly, I think it's a lot easier to get published as a novelist, but I can't seem to stop writing screenplays.

*Was there anything that you found hard about making the transition? Or was it just like, "Oh, my gosh, I've finally found the place I belong"?*

**MA:** The difficult part is learning formatting structure of screenwriting. There's really a certain way to do it. In my opinion, you should use the preferred screenwriting software tools that the industry uses. Final Draft® is the industry standard. So I had to learn Final Draft® software, which made sure that everything looked correctly formatted. So that was the hardest part, learning that. I happened to have been in a writing group. I have a strong writing group here in Portland. And they were all screenwriters. So when I first came in with pages, they would point out how I was still writing like a novelist and I needed to make that transition. But it was easy formatting stuff. My writing does lend itself to screenwriting.

*When you've been in development, how has it been seeing the way that someone was taking what you envisioned while you were writing it and putting it into their own vision?*

**MA:** What happened with *Bitsy's Labyrinth* was my screenwriting friend Clark Kohanek, said, "I really think this novel would be a great movie. I'm going to send this to my friend who's a producer in LA." And the producer liked the novel. So he optioned it, which really means nothing unless you get paid. But it was like a soft option for nothing. I was new, so that was fine by me.

The producer told me, "I really like this novel. I need to know it can translate into a screenplay. I need to know if your voice can translate, because the voice is so strong in the novel."

So in July a couple of years ago, I got swine flu. I spent the entire week I was down writing the screenplay from the novel. And that's where all the holes showed up in the story structure. The producer still loved the concept, the characters, the story, but he started pointing out to me where the climax wasn't as climactic as it should be when, in the first act, it was more. He started pointing out all the holes in the B story, the relationship. And with him, he was so generous with his time, I didn't mind it. He made my story a lot stronger. And because he liked my story, I knew that I was in good hands. He wasn't just a cold, heartless person. It made it better. It made it stronger. And in the end, since my book hadn't been published yet, I literally rewrote my novel using my screenplay. So it was a great collaborative experience for me.

My second experience working with a producer was on his own work. My friend and I collaborated to help him revise his own screenplay. That was harder, because he was attached to his story and didn't see the holes as well as we did on structure, but it was still a nice collaborative effort. And it worked out. He used a lot of what we suggested, threw out a lot of other things we liked but he didn't.

Working on a screenplay is really interesting. A novel does finally get finished. A screenplay never seems to be finished. Or it's always revised, even up until production. During production, a character, an actor will say, "This doesn't sound right to me." And on the fly, it's different. So you have no idea. It's such a collaborative event. I kind of like that though. To me, it makes it a better piece of creative art when you have more hands on it.

*The part about the other writer taking it more personally. How do you move beyond taking it personal?*

**MA:** I do take some things personally. I'm a sensitive soul—believe me. But when it comes to this writing thing, if you don't put that aside, you're not going to get anywhere. You're not going to grow as a writer or as a person if you take everything personally.

I guess you just get better with experience. And if you put enough words on the page, you start to realize it's a business. You can pour your creative energy into it, but if you get too attached, you're not going to survive because it's a business, ultimately. And people either respond or not respond. My novel that I published hardly sold. But the people who read it, loved it. Deeply moved. And that's why you do it.

*Yeah. Absolutely.*

**MA:** I'm a true codependent. I want everyone to like me. I want to please people. I want to help and be loyal. And it's growth to be able to move beyond that. So that's my therapy class for you.

*We all need it. That's probably part of what draws us to writing.*

**MA:** It's so therapeutic.

It really is. I like to think I'm a spiritual person. And my writing, for me, is a way to serve a higher purpose. The story itself. That helps, too, to not take it so personally because if I feel like I'm calling on my Higher Power every morning to help me with the words, I feel I can blame Him at the end of the day if people don't like it—it's not my fault. I asked for help. I'm the channel. I'm just channeling. So I don't have to take all that responsibility on. That really is how I try to look at it.

*It's always so interesting because you go into a project, and you think it's going to be this. And then you start writing and things happen that you had no idea.*

**MA:** Oh, yeah. Absolutely. That's, to me, divinely inspired. It really is. I love that. It's really important to me. And I'm one of those fundamentalists about story structure. I'm a firm believer in that, but within that framework, there's always that wiggle room to create something big and new—the unexpected. It's great.

*Yes.*

**MA:** I love writing. You're making me want to get back to my screenplay.

*Oh, what are you working on right now?*

**MA:** I'm working on a thriller. And it's really fun because I usually don't do that genre, but I'm having a blast with it. It's kind of an erotic thriller, which is even weirder for me because I don't usually go there. But I'm on my fourth draft.

I get all my ideas in the shower for some reason. Just this morning, I had this idea in the shower. Oh, I have to change this about her. I have to set her up this way, this one antagonist. Anyway, I'm really hoping it goes somewhere because I'm really excited. I've gotten the best feedback on this story.

*Yeah. That shower thing is not unusual. You can buy waterproof note-pads that suction cup in the shower so you don't lose your ideas.*

**MA:** That's a really good idea because I'm usually toweling off. I will sometimes jot it down, but I usually remember them. I get my best ideas in the shower.

*Yeah. I had read something that it's because you're out of your routine. You're doing something completely tactile. So your mind can process. So if you're stuck, go take a shower, I guess.*

*It sounds like you learned a lot about story structure when you took that screenwriting class. Is that something that you would recommend to someone else?*

**MA:** I always recommend Cynthia's screenwriting class. I highly recommend a book called *Save the Cat* by Blake Snyder. It's a great book on screenplays and in a very easy-to-read format. I also recommend Larry Brooks' book *Story Engineering*, because it's all about story structure. It's applicable for novels and screenwriting.

And then there's another book I highly recommend—actually teach based on it. It's called *Screenwriting: The Sequence Approach*. It breaks the three-act structure down into even more pieces. We find out that actual stories are not even just three acts, but they can be broken down into eight or more sequences of 12 to 15 minutes a sequence. And if you can learn what the turning points are in each of those, it makes it a lot more manageable. Instead of being overwhelmed by an entire novel, for example, or a screenplay, you just have to take those next 15 to 30 pages and create a mini arc out of that. So that really helped shape my writing. I picked that up in the last year.

Randall Jahnson is a local screenwriter here in town. He wrote *The Doors* and *The Mask of Zorro*. He's in Norway right now shooting another film he just wrote. I've been attending his classes for the last two years for support and to be critiqued by a professional.

I also highly recommend getting professional screenplay coverage by professional readers. I use Gordy Hoffman from BlueCat. Gordy runs a big screenwriting contest out of LA, and he comes to the Willamette Writers conference to teach. Danny Manus is another great script consultant down in the LA area who also comes to the conference. And then the third one is a new one I just picked up. It's called ScreenplayReaders.com. They actually give you professional coverage from production houses. I've grown so much as a writer to hear not just what my critique group thinks—and they're pretty brutal—but professionals in the industry. I received three passes on my last draft, but they gave me really good information as to why and even how I could fix it. That's invaluable.

You don't get that same service with novelists. Unfortunately, because the novel is so large and cumbersome, a lot of people don't take that on to get a good critique. So it's tough. A literary agent will help you if they have a vision for you and your writing. I had a really great agent for a long time who helped me with *Bitsy's Labyrinth*. I still consider her my literary agent, but I just don't do literary work.

*I'm interested in your current project because you say it's completely out of your normal genre. What inspired that?*

**MA:** I really struggle because this is an R-rated, erotic thriller. However, what inspired me to write this was that when I wrote *Bitsy's Labyrinth*, it was about a girl whose mom puts a labyrinth on her lavender farm and all this kind of spiritual, cool things that happen because of it. Like I said, the book didn't sell that much. However, one person called me from the coast, the head of the Labyrinth Network Northwest. And she said, "I loved your book. And I happened to notice that you live near Coffee Creek Correctional Facility." It's the only women's prison in the state of Oregon. It's for minimum, maximum. All women go to Coffee Creek.

She said, "We desperately need people to volunteer to bring a labyrinth walk into the inmates, would you be interested?" For some reason I said, "Sure." I was scared to death. I've never in my life thought I would enter a maximum security prison, but I did. It's been three years now. Now I know that's why I had to publish *Bitsy's Labyrinth*. I had to go through the humiliation of no sales and no deal because that was what I'm supposed to do.

So fast forward now. The idea comes up that my protagonist in this thriller is a recovering alcoholic who takes meetings into Coffee Creek because I know it intimately now. And she has a secret gambling addiction. I know from Coffee Creek there are a lot of women there who had gambling addictions, who embezzled money and got caught, and now they're in jail. I've been intimate enough with these inmates to understand that. So my story is about a recovering alcoholic with a secret gambling addiction whose husband's co-worker is sexually blackmailing her. And then he ends up getting murdered, and they all think she did it. So she has to find the true killer.

All of that came from my experience at Coffee Creek. It took me out of my norm. And I had to meditate on it. Is this really what I'm supposed to be writing?

The more I get to know those women, the more I see just how human they are. These are not vicious inmates like you think. Part of our training was to read the book *Orange is the New Black*. It's a lot like that. Just last week, I got my hair done at the Coffee Creek salon because I'm badged and I can go in. They have a salon program. The inmate who does my hair and nails? I would be really close friends with her on the outside. She's going to be there 18 years.

*Wow.*

**MA:** That's why you break out of your norm. You experience something new, and you write something new. I guess that's the short answer.

*It does sound like that was a hugely powerful experience. Have you had other experiences like that, that just pulled you out of what you normally do that have inspired you in that way? It would be hard to really liken anything else to that because that is so different than any of our regular, everyday lives.*

**MA:** My memoir was about personal experience. It was about all the ways I don't stay in the moment. Everyone always writes about being "in the moment," so it was a funny take on that. What was out of my comfort zone for that was to personally expose myself so much. I even wrote about trying a Brazilian waxing. I learned lessons about how much of myself to reveal in my work. I would never write a memoir now.

I always usually try to make my writing inspirational, but I don't know how I'm going to get that going with the thriller. I am hoping it'll inspire people who have addiction issues.

*Addictions like gambling and sex addiction, I feel like they're even harder for people to be open about than substance addictions because people say, "Well, why don't you just stop doing it?"*

**MA:** Definitely. And living in Oregon, it's so much harder to stay away from gambling because of the video lottery games everywhere. It's a real problem for people who have access at every corner. Gambling addicts before would just have to stay away from Vegas. And then it was, "stay away from the Indian casino." Here in Oregon, you can't go past Shari's down the block without worrying about whether you're going to go in and gamble. So that's another reason I am so passionate about this screenplay. I actually applied for the Oregon Fellowship to write the screenplay, thinking I wanted it to have a statement on Oregon's gambling. I really hope, if it gets produced, that it'll be produced in Oregon by someone who cares.

I want viewers to be educated on what goes on in Oregon, both in the lottery and also the women's prison, what makes up the women's prison. We only have one. Isn't that funny? I think it's amazing that DUI people and murderers are in the same place. It's kind of crazy.

*Wow. I was wondering what advice you'd have for someone who wants to navigate the business of screenwriting.*

**MA:** It's really important to get involved and to be of service. The best way to be in the middle of the crowd is to offer your help. That's what I've always done. I started with the conference because I had training and development skills as a background in my career before I became a stay-at-home mom. I offered to the president that I could help her build her curriculum because I knew what training and development looked like. Selfishly, I got something out of it, all these connections. I got to personally email authors, agents, managers, and producers. But I did want to give back. If we always have that attitude of giving back, then you can meet the right people.

Beyond that, you should be in a writer's group that is connected. I would try to avoid groups where everyone's a beginner and no one has a connection because no one will learn. It's the blind leading the blind. And then I would refer back to those coverage people I gave you, the LA people with the coverage. Professional coverage is really good because you get in front of industry people. And screenwriting contests, because even though you might not elevate to first place, your name is in front of some real power people in the industry. *Bitsy's Labyrinth*, the screenplay, made it to the top 100 in Scriptapalooza, one of the bigger contests. It's been marketed by them because they'll do that for the top 100. I haven't gotten a call, but I know several people have read that script. So people may know my name from that, people I don't even know yet.

Same with paying Danny or Gordy or ScreenplayReaders, they all know who I am. And if they like something, they'll pass it on, because that's good business for them. So that's how I would break in. The biggest overarching goal would be to show your work to people. If you're one of those writers who have a hard time giving it up until you think it's perfect, you're never, ever going to show anyone anything. In screenwriting, you have to just lay it all out there. People are brutal. But that's in every business. It's not just screenwriting. But it seems like in screenwriting, the people you deal with are a lot less forgiving. And in screenwriting, you have to be a chameleon. I'm a middle-aged woman trying to crack a market that's predominantly run by young men in their twenties. It's not for the faint of heart. You have to believe in doing it without even ever expecting to get produced.

*How can you keep your motivation up knowing that it is so hard to actually get produced?*

**MA:** Well, the truth is I contemplate quitting all the time. I do. I get discouraged just like everyone else. I think, "What else can I do? What else can I create? I need to create. Maybe I'll start a business. Maybe I'll do this." I do that all the time. "What's my alternative?" But it always comes back to that fact that this is what I have to do. If you're doing some meditation or quiet time and it's what you're always called to do, then you just have to keep doing it.

And get a support group who gets you. In my writing group, each individual at one time or another has walked into the group to say, "I can't do this anymore. I have to do something else." We just let them feel that, let them go through it. They keep coming back, so I know I'm not unique in that regard. It's comforting to be able to relate to other writers who share that because it's so tough. That's how I do it. I have good writing buddies, and I meditate on it. And I keep coming back.

"I get my best ideas in
the shower."

— *Mary Andonian*

# 2  Patricia Briggs

Patricia Briggs is the #1 New York Times best selling author of the Mercy Thompson series and has written 22 novels to date; she is currently writing novel number twenty three. Patty began her career writing traditional fantasy novels in 1993, and shifted gears in 2006 to write urban fantasy. *Moon Called* was the first of her signature series about Mercy Thompson. The non-stop adventure left readers wanting more of this exciting new urban fantasy series about a shape-shifting mechanic spread quickly. The series has continued to grow in popularity with the release of each book. Patty also writes the Alpha and Omega series, which are set in the same world as the Mercy Thompson novels; what began as a novella expanded into a full new series, all of which debuted on the NY Times bestsellers list as well.

Patty and her family reside in Eastern Washington near Tri-Cities, home of Mercy Thompson—yes, it's a real place! When not working on the next book, she can be found playing truant out in her horse pastures, playing with the newest babies. For more information about Patricia Briggs and her marvelous novels, visit the author on the web at www.patriciabriggs.com or on Facebook.

---

*I'm interested in how you have kind of woven where you live and the mythology of the Northwest into your books.*

**Patricia Briggs:** Geography plays so much importance when you're world-building, especially traditional fantasy, but also urban fantasy, because urban fantasy, you know, it's the werewolves and vampires. Part of the character is the real world. You take these fantastical elements and stick them in the real world, so the real world has to be real solid. So it's much easier to work with places where I live. When I was writing *Dragon Bones* and *Dragon Blood*, which are probably the most geographically influenced books in the traditional fantasy that I wrote, the main character came from a place just like Montana where the weather is cold and harsh and people really get down to the basics. Survival is big. What color you wear is not big. So that helped. But with the urban fantasy, in a way it's even more important, because to me, the magic of urban fantasy happens with this juxtaposition of the fantastic on the real place.

My publisher asked me to write an urban fantasy, and what they gave me was, they needed a female protagonist, involved with werewolves and vampires, with a complicated love life. She didn't have to be one of the preternatural critters, but she had to be involved in that community, which was really kind of a very open thing, and to me, that's kind of the basis of what urban fantasy is, although it's evolved somewhat since then.

So I looked around and said okay, well, I have to set it in a place I know really well. We were living here in the Tri-Cities, eastern Washington State, and I thought about Spokane, which I know pretty well. I thought about Seattle, and this is before all of our Seattle writers did urban fantasy set in Seattle. It's the most common urban-fantasy setting at this point, but nobody was doing it then. We had Jim Butcher in Chicago, which I also know, but he was already there. Then St. Louis for Hamilton and Kim Harrison who was set in Cincinnati. Charlaine Harris was the only one not doing it in a big urban center, but she was doing it in a small town in the South.

So I looked at Spokane. Spokane I could have just done, because I grew up in Montana, and Spokane is the big city if you grew up in Montana. Seattle, I would have had to come over and do a lot more research—in fact, I did that later.

But as I was sitting there looking around, I realized the Tri-Cities is one of the most unique environments I have seen, because it has the Pacific Northwest Laboratory and all of the big government-contracted companies here. The overall political leaning is very conservative, right, but it's a different kind of conservative than you find other places, like eastern Washington State just because Richland, which is one of the Tri-Cities, has more PhDs per capita than any other city in the U.S.

It's a very educated right-wing environment, which is really unusual. That group just tends to be less academic, right?

If you talk to somebody from the Tri-Cities, they will tell you that this is a white, Anglo-Saxon, Protestant community that is very heavily Christian and all this stuff. Then you walk into the mall, and you hear 40 different languages in 15 different colors and nobody sees them. And it's not that they don't see the individual, they don't see the fact that these people are different than they are. Because they're educated enough not to be scared of people who are different.

So it amuses me that I walk through this community, which is red, yellow, black, white, infinite languages, infinite colors, and nobody cares. Nobody notices, and I think they would not notice vampires and werewolves either. So that's why I used it. That's why I set the urban fantasies in here. It's a very Tri-Cities thing.

But I kind of feel like the idea that if there were vampires and werewolves around that they would live in a place like the Pacific Northwest as very plausible. The Pacific Northwest has room to run. If you're a werewolf, you need room to run, right?

*Definitely.*

**PB:** The West, as opposed to the East, we lived in Chicago, and people in Chicago would shoot me for calling them Easterners, they're Midwesterners, but it felt very alien and very eastern. They get in your face. They're nosy. They know who their neighbors are, and they tell you how to do your laundry at the laundromat, and all sorts of things, right? But in the West, you never do that. In the West, there's this idea that came out of the western experience, right, that whole expansion to the West, that you don't ask people questions that they don't offer. You don't poke into people's business. You're polite, which to us means that if somebody says "does this make me look fat?" you look at them and you say, "oh, it's a pretty color, but maybe this would look better." In the East, they'd say, "Yeah, that makes you look fat." Or they'd say, "No, your butt makes you look fat."

If you're a New Yorker, and you talk to somebody from California, you feel like they lie to you all the time, and if you're from California and you go to New York, you think they're so rude. But the West environment is a much better environment for a group of people who are trying to hide themselves.

So this is from the writing angle, from the setting stories angle. If you're setting magical realism or magical things, the West actually seems like a place that you would see more of the preternatural community because there's more room for them, and there's more room for them to hide.

Now, as a writer, a busy urban life would get in my way. It's too easy to distract myself, and I like living in the Pacific Northwest where I can go out and be in nature. It renews my spirit. It's like drinking at the well of creativity. It takes me out of the mundane, takes me out of my daily life, and puts me in a place where I can create.

*So I think it's interesting that your publisher asked you to make that shift. Did that make it harder or easier, do you think, than if you'd come up with it yourself?*

**PB:** At the time, there were only a few people writing urban fantasy, as it exists now.

Tanya Huff wrote The Blood Books about 10 years before. In fact, when I met Tanya Huff, I said "tell me what you're writing now so I know what to write 10 years from now," because she's the best. She's awesome.

But at the time, really, it was kind of that noir horror crossed with fantasy. And that was pretty much Laurell Hamilton's thing. Then Charlaine wrote a book, the first Sookie book, and Jim Butcher wrote *Storm Front*, his first book. I can't remember the names of my books, but I remember theirs.

Kim Harrison wrote *Dead Witch Walking*, and also Kelley Armstrong had written *Bitten*, but they were pretty isolated. I loved them, and I read them, but I would not have jumped in there because I would have felt like I was jumping in somebody else's pond without permission to go play. But I had just finished a hundred and twenty-thousand-word fantasy in three months, and I was pretty burned out on traditional fantasy. If I had to describe another room that really wasn't here I would have broken out in tears. It was really hard.

I did it to myself. It was not my publisher's fault. But I was really burned out, and I was just getting ready to call my editor and say you know, I think I'm going to have to take six months off because I don't think I can write another word. That was when she called me and said we just lost a bidding war for an urban fantasy writer, and urban fantasy seems to be the only bright spot. This was after 9/11, and the publishing industry really kind of crashed. They are right there in downtown Manhattan, and they walked by that every day, and it created this kind of a real malaise in the publishing industry right there that lingered and still lingers a little bit now. The book industry is right now in a changing time, and the only happy spot they had found was in urban fantasy.

My editor is Anne Sowards, and she's just the bomb. She's the nicest woman in the entire world, and she's so incredibly smart, she's just great. Her boss said to her, "Don't we have any of our writers who can write this stuff?"

Anne called me and she said "I know you like to read urban fantasy, can you write them?" And I said yes.

So she gave me that, I sat down, and within a week, I had about a hundred pages written, which is really not something I do. I can do it at the end of a book, but I very seldom do it at the beginning of a book because I'm too busy setting things up. And to go from I don't think I can write another word to just, boom, was really fun.

So actually it didn't hurt anything at all that they had asked me. If I had not enjoyed the genre, if they asked me to do something like a hard science-fiction novel, I would have said no. I've been in this business long enough to know that writers who try to write things because they think they're going to sell and not because they love the genre, fail, because readers know. Readers can tell when your heart's not in it.

*Speaking of putting your heart into it, do you ever have to make a boundary with yourself because you're putting too much?*

**PB:** Maureen McHugh, I think, said in *Locus*, many, many years ago, that writing is like fan dancing in public. Fan dancing is an old burlesque show where you would be naked and you would dance with great big feather fans. Everybody in the audience would watch to see if they could see skin, and you're trying to keep most of your body covered. But a good fan dancer showed people enough skin, and maybe they thought they were seeing more skin than they actually were, but not so much that you were standing naked in public.

I really love that quote because I think that's right. So if you don't show your skin at all, the book has no meat, it has no depth. It could be a good book. It could be a fun book. But it's not a book that's going to stick with readers. It's not a book that's going to make readers go back, I have to find that author again. They're just not going to do that. So you have to give them enough skin.

But yeah, I do boundaries. I'm not my characters. My characters are good friends of mine. I go out and play with my imaginary friends all the time, but if I find that I'm making a character too much like myself, I back off and try something else. For one thing, it's not as much fun. I was in drama in high school, and a little bit in college, and I really love being somebody else. I love stepping into a completely different character. Those kinds of things are really fun, and as a writer, that's one of the things that drives me to writers. I love to see the inside of somebody else's brain and try to figure out, take it apart, and figure out how they work.

So I don't really have the impulse to put myself in these situations. And it helps writing fantasy instead of romance, where you have to put yourself in it a little bit more. So writing fantasy, I can put my best friends in, and we can have fun. For instance, Mercy. I'm not a car mechanic. My husband can turn a good wrench, so I'll use his stories. And we always had Volkswagens.

So you have to use things you know, the fun little things. We had a Vanagon and the electric started being weird, and we took it to our local mechanic who was just awesome. I based Zee off him. He was just a really fun guy. We told him our electric has gone freaky, like the lights on the left-hand side of the van don't work sometimes and sometimes they do. He looked at us and he said, "Have you rotated your fuses?" And we looked at him and asked if that was a blinker-fluid thing. That's one of the big jokes mechanics will play on people who don't know anything about cars—you drive in and you go my turn signals aren't working, and they'll say have you checked your blinker fluid? But he said no, no, no. European cars, the old Volkswagens, all had copper fuses, and if you have them in a wet environment for very long, they'll develop a verdigris. The way to get rid of that is to rotate them in the socket. Then they get a good connection again, and that's what you need. So those kinds of stories you only get when you live them, so you have to pull things from your life.

But, I pick and choose. The funny things, weird things, uncomfortable things, I use. Personal things, I don't use.

My characters, a lot of them have conflicts with their parents, and I can do that because I didn't have any. My parents were just awesome. Or they have problems with their in-laws, and I can do that because my in-laws just rock, and they know that I think that. But for instance, I have a daughter who's got some health issues that have led to some other issues, and I don't use that at all, because that's personal, and that doesn't belong in there. I have a friend who was stalked and someday I'm going to use it, but I'm not going to use it in any way that's going to bother her. And the guy who stalked her has passed away, so that's not going to bother him.

Things that are too close to people who are experiencing the pain right now, I try not to use in my book at all. I don't base characters on people I know with one exception, two exceptions, three exceptions. Okay, sorry, three exceptions.

Two of them were done with permission. One of them, a friend of mine came up and said Mercy needs to get information from an antiquarian bookseller, because he was an antiquarian bookseller, and he said you have to put me in your book, and then, in the next couple of books, I ran into a situation where I needed to do that. So that's what I did. I put him in there. Then the next book, I thought I was going to have to kill him, so I called him up, and I said okay, Jess, and I had to change his name, because his name's Jess, like Adam's daughter's name is Jesse. So I said, okay, I had to change Jessie, I had to change…he's not based on you anymore, because I might have to kill him, and he said, "No, no, that's okay. You can kill him." But that's why I don't base characters on people I know. Because then I might have to kill them.

The other one is Zee. He's kind of Mercy's teacher. He taught her mechanic work and things like that, and Mercy bought the mechanic shop from him.

He is based really heavily on our old friend who was a mechanic here in the Tri-Cities. Anybody who's had Volkswagens in Tri-Cities knows who he is and can see it. He was just such a character, and as soon as I knew I was going to write these Mercy books, I asked him, "Do you mind if I steal you for my book? Is that okay?" He was really flattered. He was dying from lung cancer. I knew that at the time, which is one of the reasons, probably, that I did it. He died before the books came out.

Then the third one is a guy my husband worked with at the Shedd Aquarium in Chicago. He worked there for a year as an aquarist, and one of his fellow aquarists was this guy who was like six foot five, six foot six. He was perfectly handsome, but he just looked as if you wanted to speak in short sentences when you talked to him, you know, kind of help him along. And he wore these rollerblades.

The Shedd is set up so that the people who came in to see the fish, their path was a fork, right, but the aquarists who were working behind the scenes had this huge area in the back to get from one to the other because it was behind all of the big tanks, right. He used to wear his rollerblades at the Shedd and come around the outside. It's a circle, so you cannot see too far ahead of you. So he's going about 15 miles an hour on this, and in order to let people know he's coming, he sings, and he sings "dope de dope, de dope dope dope dope" from the old Looney Tunes cartoon. And he would stretch out his arms and flap them as he went. And he was awesome. He was brilliant, absolutely brilliant, and it would take people by surprise, and it just delighted me, that idea that somebody who is huge and handsome but not-too-bright looking, and people treated him like he belonged on the short bus, and he was brilliant, and he took great delight in people treating him like that, and I thought I have to do it.

So I did it for a minor character in an early book, *Steal the Dragon*, and then I had so much fun with that character that I modified it again, and used him for the main character in *Dragon Bone*s and *Dragon Blood* just because, as a writer, I really like having secrets with readers. It's really fun, it's a fun thing to do. That's a secret of spy novels. And of *Lord of the Rings* because when you read *Lord of the Rings* for the fifteenth time, you know all the secret names for Minas Tirith. And when he just casually mentions it, you know what it is, and you know that half the readers don't. It's like an in-game. It makes you feel like part of the group.

My favorite scene I ever wrote, because I had so much fun doing it, was in *Dragon Bones*. They're trying to catch a horse—there's a stallion in with a mare. And they're trying and trying to catch the stallion. So he walks out with a bucket of grain and catches the mare, and of course, the stallion, who's running from everybody else, goes where the mare's going. So he walks up to his uncle, and he looks his uncle straight in the face, and he says, "The secret of catching a horse is you have to be smarter than the horse." And he says that knowing that his uncle does not think he's smarter than a horse.

So those are the three characters I stole from real life. But one of my boundaries is that I don't base characters on real live people, and in 22 books, I've had three characters. I usually have casts of thousands, so I think that's pretty good.

I will say that I steal bits and pieces. I don't have any problem stealing bits and pieces, but I never use that for the whole character.

*One of the things I wanted to talk to you about is success as a writer. Sometimes, I think that even though writers will say that they fear failure, a lot of times what they fear is success.*

**PB:** I know that I feel extraordinarily lucky, extraordinarily lucky that it was not my first book that made it big. I'd been writing for 15 years when the Mercy books made it big.

Before that, it was just a nice hobby. Most people's hobbies cost them money, but my hobby usually paid for itself. I read a lot of books, and we buy computers and upgrade every two or three years so I can keep writing. Then we used to use any excess to buy our cars, which were generally VWs with one-hundred-thousand-plus miles on them, because you don't make a whole lot of money in the mid-list, especially anymore.

It was just a nice hobby, and by the time that it hit big, I had enough experience to know that it wasn't particularly me, that it was the good-luck publishing fairy. I didn't parade around and say how great I am, how great I am, because I knew better.

If you are a young writer and you have your first book go big, the temptation is to really take that upon yourself. I think successful books have to be well written. Well, maybe not well written, but have good storytelling, which is different.

I have a list of authors whose books I keep picking up because they sound so interesting. And they're so well written. Perfect grammar and beautiful word choices and all that stuff. But they don't tell good stories. They don't know how to put together tension, and they don't know how to make characters you like and care about.

Storytelling is more important to be a successful writer than craftsmanship, although craftsmanship helps, and it certainly helps repeatability.

I know that when the books became successful there was a lot of pressure for the next one to be a successful book, and I had to just tune it out. For the first four or five books in the Mercy series, I would just pretend that the checks that came had nothing to do with the books I was writing. It was, like, I had won the lottery, you know what I mean, that kind of thing? Oh, look, that's a nice check, but I have to get this book written because I told people I'd write it. If I let myself think about it, then the books try to become too important, and they would lose their energy.

Writing is like this. You have to believe two different things at the same time, all the time, and after a while you get really good at it. So I can believe, one, that my writing sucks, and two, that people want to read it anyway, at the same time, because I have to in order to fix what's wrong with the story, you have to believe there was something wrong with the story, but in order to get any desire at all to write, you have to believe that somebody else will want to read it.

So believing two opposite things at the same time is kind of your bread and butter as a writer. So believing that the money that came in response to the contracts I signed had nothing to do with the books. It was just some money coming in.

*I know that pressure has halted so many people's careers.*

**PB:** Right. I'm very happy where I'm at. I'm not sure that I would like to be where Charlaine Harris is. Or poor Stephenie Meyer. Or J.K. Rowling. I don't want to be there. I'm very grateful to them because they increased the readers in our genre, but it's very nice that I'm not famous-famous.

*You autofill when someone searches in Google, but you're not first on the list. That's got to be a pretty good place.*

**PB:** The cool thing is that the money the books make right now lets me live very comfortably. I can write them at the speed I am comfortable, so that I know the books are different from each other. I'm not forced to write the same book over and over again. It supports my horse habit.

*Horses are not cheap.*

**PB:** That's right, I'm breeding Arabians. And the best way to get a small fortune with horse breeding is to start with a large one. The kids can go to college, and I don't worry about the monthly bills. I feel very lucky to be where I am.

I thought I'd point out, too, that success in writing, everybody's meter is different, right? I feel like I was a successful writer because I could publish everything I wrote and for me, for many years, that was awesome, and I felt very comfortable there. The explosion from the Mercy Thompson series I did was fun. But it was pretty scary, too. A lot of things in our lives changed pretty fast. Some things were very nice, and some things were very uncomfortable.

I like to go to parties if it's somebody else's birthday party. That's really fun. My own birthday party is really uncomfortable. So going to science fiction conventions changed a lot. It used to be I could go to science fiction conventions, and I was just hanging out with my buddies. You know, my best friends I saw three times a year. Now when I go to science fiction conventions, I really...it's all work. It's really hard to get half an hour, 45 minutes with my friends. It's fine, but it was a big change. And for me, it was kind of uncomfortable because I don't crave being the center of attention. I'm pretty used to it, it's okay now, but it's not something I look for.

I kind of think that there are a lot of writers like me because you don't get a career of sitting by yourself in an office for eight to 10 hours a day. You don't do that to yourself if you like being out among people, right? There are certainly exceptions. I mean, Jay Lake is an awesome people person. But I do know that a lot of people can go out and enjoy conventions, but they come home and they lock themselves in their room and don't talk to anybody for a week. That can be very uncomfortable for some writers.

*If you had some advice for someone who wanted to tell a great story, where would you tell them to look? What authors should they read? Where should they focus their improvement of their craft?*

**PB:** For me, I write what I really like to read, and I like to read character-focused stories. When I started writing, I looked to them and I said I can write either romance or fantasy — that's what I read the most. I just didn't think I could pay attention to a romance long enough to write a book, and as it turned out, it was a very good choice, fantasy was for me.

As a writer, you have to read and push your boundaries. Read things that you would not normally read. A few years ago, I joined a book club when I was living in Montana because I wanted to kind of expand my horizon. My favorite reads are the books that hit *New York Times*. Nora Roberts I love, especially as J.D. Robb. So I push my boundaries a little bit and went kind of literary with it, or the Oprah books, which I never normally would read.

So expand your boundaries. Read all over the place and see where you really like. What genre really does it for you? But you have to read, and you have to go out and find your space.

Once you have that, then you start writing, and you see where you are coming up short. "Oh, look, I have problems with conversation. I don't know how to write a conversation so it sounds natural. So who do I read that has good conversations?" When I wrote Masques, I went to Dick Francis, who wrote horse-racing mysteries, but his conversations are really good. The people feel real. They conduct information, but they do a lot of information in very short order. You get a lot of personality, and you get a lot of mystery information, you get a lot in these very short conversations.

Read. Read a lot. Read books that you hate and figure out why you hate them. Is it the voice? For me, voice is very important. I can read a book on, I don't know, on the Cold War, which scares me and it's not a happy place. I can read a book on the Cold War if it's well written. I can read a book on planting corn if it's well written. So voice is very important to me, but it may not be to somebody else who's trying to write. Maybe what they really like is taking science and making a story out of it. Whatever floats your boat is fine. But find somebody who's doing it well, figure out what you like about it, and borrow their toolbox. And find somebody who's not doing it well and figure out why you don't like it, right?

Workshops are very valuable, but you have to be careful and take only as much out of it as is useful. Never go to a workshop expecting someone to pat you on the head and say good job, good job, because they just won't do that, because it's not their job.

At the same time, if somebody tells you you can't write, don't even try, ignore them. True story. A friend of mine in a writers' group, and I'm not going to give names, but a friend of mine in a writers' group was just incredibly well educated about writing, and he would talk about writing, and I would think oh, wow, he just knows so much, and I learned so much from him. Then he put a piece in this workshop, and I went, this is him? Holy cow, this is awful. This is terrible. It reads like a high schooler wrote it, and he knows so much, how does he do this?

But he gradually got better and better and then he went on to win the Writers of the Future contest and is now publishing all over the place, and he's a fan-damn-tastic writer. So I don't ever believe it is proper to tell somebody they can't write, because it's not true. Everybody is in a different place on their journey, right, and if it's important enough to them, they'll get there. If it's not important enough to them, they'll have fun along the way, and they'll learn something. You know, like any great hobby, it serves a purpose. It may be to get you out of your everyday world. It may be to fulfill your dreams. So go ahead and write, that's fine. But never believe anybody who tells you you can't write. That's my other little piece of advice.

My favorite thing to do when I feel really discouraged about my own writing, I read a review of *To Kill a Mockingbird*, which is one of my favorite books, where they just pan it. They hated it, just absolutely hated it, and I read that one. Then Ursula K. Le Guin has published on her website the rejection letter she got for *The Left Hand of Darkness*. She blacked out names, there are no names, where they tell her that maybe someday she'll be a real writer, and this piece shows promise but it's not there yet.

Find things that will encourage you. Find things that make you want to write stories. My big inspiration is the *Lord of the Rings* movies. The Peter Jackson *Lord of the Rings* movies. Whenever I feel like my well has gone dry, and I just don't have any more stories to tell, because now, as a writer, as a "successful" writer, I push my muse all the time, right. I don't have the luxury of sitting around and waiting until the muse says oh, let's write a story. I do it every day. It's been years since I've actually sat down and watched all three movies back to back, because I'm really afraid of losing the magic, but I can hop in anywhere in that story, anywhere, and watch 10 or 15 minutes and I'm ready to go tell stories again, because Peter caught that magic. It's not just Peter Jackson. It's all of the actors and all of the people who put the sets together. They just made this incredibly rich, beautiful world that is as renewing to my writing muse as walking out in the mountains and forests is to my spiritual muse, right? For me, it works, and I'm really afraid to lose that, so when I'm not looking for inspiration I don't watch it.

But look for those things. Balance is important, too, especially as you become more successful as a writer. The temptation is to sit down and write and let it consume you. But you can't do that, because eventually you won't have anything to write. Without experiencing your life, you can't write about it. All you can do is rehash what other people say or what you've said before.

For me, it pushes me to create balance, because writing is all internal, and I do it in an office, and I'm shut away from the outside, and I don't have any windows that look outside because it's too distracting. I write in a little construction trailer. The horses are a balance to that, because the horses are all external. I'm outside. I'm doing physical things. I'm interacting. And it helps me to keep a healthy balance.

When I was in high school—and this was back in the early days, when we were programming in Basic—I had computer classes and I loved them. I would look up from programming and four or five hours would have passed and it felt like 10 minutes.

Writing is the same way. When I get into it, I'll look up and oh, my gosh, I've been doing this for…I've been working on this thing for eight hours. How did that happen? Or sometimes, I'll look up and it's two o'clock in the morning and I'll have been working on the thing for 15 hours.

It creates an unhealthy thing where the fantasy world becomes more real than the real world. It's really important to get out and do things and not let yourself get shut in your little world that you're creating. I have been on panels with people who I think needed to quit writing because they quit dealing with the real world. The characters that they created were more real to them than the people around them, and I just don't think that's healthy. First of all, I don't think you can write well. I don't think you can write a good book from that perspective. But more importantly, I don't think that you can be a healthy human being from that perspective either.

*Sounds like you've learned a ton about yourself through writing. Is there anything else writing has taught you?*

**PB:** You have to have a pretty clear view of who you are and where you are when you write, and I will say that it depends on where you want to write.

If you're writing genre fiction, if you want to write popular genre fiction, then you have to kind of share the mores of your society, the idea that people who do bad things need to be stopped. It doesn't always work in the real world, but justice has to prevail in fiction. One of the reasons people read books and watch movies is just that they can feel like there is a place in the world, in a fantasy world, in between the pages of a book, in which justice prevails, in which good triumphs over evil.

If you are the kind of person who does not have the mores of your society, in which you think that it's okay for drug dealers to sell to little kids, pedophilia is an okay hobby, you know, people like that cannot write books people will want to read in the long run. They might be able to get it for a shock value. They might be able to even get literary fiction, but you're not going to get a big readership, unless you're pretty normal. As normal as writers can get.

The other thing is that you have to understand people. Writers have to understand people, and if you don't understand people, you cannot write a book. Pattern recognition, to me, is just fascinating. When I was in college, one of my professor's son was a PhD in computer science. This was back in the 80s, and they were talking about artificial intelligence. He said the most difficult thing was teaching computers to be intelligent because computers don't do pattern recognition. For example, if somebody draws Mickey Mouse, they don't have to draw much of Mickey Mouse for people to recognize it. But a computer will look at it and say that's five lines on the board. Most people can read between the lines, and if your characters do not act like real people, they'll notice it. They may or may not know what's wrong. They may or may not know how to fix it. They just know that this is not a fun read. I don't believe in these people. I don't believe in your world because your people don't act like people.

So one of the things you have to do, as a writer, is understand how people work. Acting classes will do you more good than writing classes in a lot of ways, especially to start out, because in acting class, you have to be somebody you're not, step into somebody else's shoes, and it's guided, because you have the play, and famous plays are famous because they're very good at getting inside people's heads. Even if you don't want to get out on stage, go take some acting classes.

"I don't base characters on
people I know.
Because then I might
have to kill them."

*— Patricia Briggs*

# 3 J. Anderson Coats

J. Anderson Coats writes historical fiction set in the middle ages that routinely includes too much violence, name-calling and petty vandalism perpetrated by badly-behaved young people. Her first book, *The Wicked and the Just*, came out 17 April 2012. She studied history at Bryn Mawr College, where she graduated magna cum laude with departmental honors. She also holds a master's degree in library and information science from Drexel University and a master's degree in history from the University of Washington. Currently, Jillian lives in the Pacific Northwest in a hundred-year-old house with her husband, teenage son, and a cat with thumbs. On a clear day, she can see the Olympic mountains from her front window. On the foggy ones, she can smell the Puget Sound.

---

*What's your story? What inspires you?*

**J. Anderson Coats:** If the question is what inspired *The Wicked and the Just* that's a totally different question than what inspires me to write in general.

The word inspire, for me, doesn't work because the literal Latin is to breathe in and to me that implies that creativity and writing comes from somewhere outside. Like the muse comes and sprinkles the pixie dust and then oh, hooray I see it now. And for me, writing is not that. It's more of a compulsion and it comes from my deep gaudy core and it is something that needs to come out rather than something that comes from outside and comes in and has to cycle through. It's basically like, I can't not write. It's how I interface with the world. It's how I process things that happen to me that are either good or bad. It comes out in various ways but you know fiction's one of the ways it comes out and that's, that's really kind of, you know that's not inspire. That's something else.

*When you're feeling the compulsion to get a new story out there, how does that feel?*

**JAC:** It feels, often it feels like an exorcism. Again, me and the Latin, to cut out of. Very often it's like I have this idea or thought that's floating around in my head and it's a response to something, something I've read, something I've seen. And it sort of takes form and starts, you know, a character will start talking to me and very often it feels like it's something that I need out of my head and out of my dark gaudy core, I guess. And it feels almost like putting down a heavy back pack, where something is just everything feels different, almost lighter. And then you realize that you've produced this thing that took a chunk of you with it, and that's often very good.

*I like that. Like just getting a big weight off. What about* The Wicked and the Just? *Where did that one come from?*

**JAC:** That's kind of convoluted. I was the kind of geeky teenager that had research interests. And one of my very first ones, I was probably 13 or 14, was I wondered why Wales didn't have a tradition of resistance against English rule the way Ireland and Scotland did. And by the time I realized that wasn't particularly correct, and it was really bad history, I'd done enough research to sort of cherry pick this event, this rebellion, out of early colonial Wales and I started writing.

I wrote a whole book about it, about the rebellion itself, and I ended up always having to go back and refer to why the rebels were so angry. And then I realized that the conditions that lead up to the rebellion were just as interesting as the rebellion itself. I wanted to write about that. And that was the story that eventually became *The Wicked and The Just.*

*So that one has been with you for a long time.*

**JAC:** It has. It rose from my adolescent desire for there to have been some kind of counter revolution to the conquest of Wales and the fall of native government. And it just wasn't forthcoming, it just didn't happen. All the native nobility were actually happy because they really didn't like one another very much. There was a lot of infighting among the native nobility and the native government. So they were really happy to stab their prince in the back. They were happy to see him go.

And then when they realized what they got in return wasn't going to go away as easily, there was not that same cycle of well, we just don't like you so we're going to have a Russian election and get rid of you, it was much more permanent. By the time they realized that, the new government was installed, it wasn't going away. I was very discouraged by that. I didn't understand why resistance didn't happen. I had to dig real deep. It was hard for teenage me to really appreciate what was going on, and it took grown-up me to write that story.

*Sometimes you need that perspective on things. What is the greatest writing lesson you learned in getting* The Wicked and the Just *out there?*

**JAC:** It wasn't so much a lesson that I learned, but it was one that really got cemented in my head. I'd kind of understood before but I didn't really grok until this happened. And that was something I got from a fantasy writer named Elizabeth Bair, who told me she got it from Neil Gaiman, and he attributed it to a guy named Gene Wolfe.

Learn to write this book. You never learn how to write novels. You learn how to write this one particular novel. I've always kind of been suspicious of structure. Not that I think it's bad to have a plot. But I don't think there's a formula you can follow. You just have x happen by page 20 and y happen by page 50 and then have the big reveal on page 175, everything will be okay and it will all fall into place, and it makes it easy. It's very comforting to think that that's all it takes to write a book. But I really have come to see it as more like tools in a toolbox. When you're writing this particular book, maybe you really need a hammer because you're always hammering in nails. But then you're done with it and you try to write the next one. You try to use your hammer but you find out you really need a screwdriver this time, and not just a standard one. You need that weird little star with the nose on the end. It takes a very specialized tool. If you're not willing to put your hammer down long enough to find the tool you need, your books are either all going to sound the same or you're just going to bang your head against a wall when you can't make the plot do what you want. The characters won't do what you want. You can't figure out a way to make them do what you want. And it's just an exercise in frustration.

When you approach it like tools in a toolbox, you really have to fig-ure out what the book needs. If you don't already have that tool in your toolbox, you learn the skill that you need. If you do, then you need to dust it off and try it until you find what is going to work for this particular book. Because there is no formula. There is no magic thing. And that's really the biggest thing I learned. Trust the process, and don't get too wrapped up in structure and in making sure that you're following somebody else's directives. Do what the book needs.

*Was there anything in particular that you remember with* The Wicked and the Just *that you had to go find somewhere?*

**JAC:** The book I wrote right before it had three different narrator points of view. And I remember getting a lot of feedback from people saying no these are too close together, that the voices are too similar. And I thought I'm never writing another multiple perspective book. It's just not going to happen. It's just too much trouble.

And I started writing *The Wicked and the Just* from one of the character's point of view and I got partway into it and I realized I needed somebody from either side of this to really tell the story properly, to go where I want to take it.

So I had to bite the bullet and accept that not only was I going to have to pull out the dual narration, but I was going to have to really make them distinct because they are drawn from such radically different communities with totally different sets of experiences. And just sort of say, okay, just suck it up and do it. I was not excited by that but I eventually came around to realizing that it was a very powerful technique, and I'm glad I did it.

*When you feel like you need help on a technique, where do you go?*

**JAC:**  I typically try to write it a bunch of different ways, I sit and think about what I need to do. I've never really been much for craft books. I know some people swear by them, you know, *Save the Cat* and *Story Engineering.* That's great for them if it helps them, but it's just never really been helpful to me. I've always found it to be a bit too prescriptive because then I get it wrapped around my axle. I think, "Oh no, I'm not doing it right. I'm deviating from the plan."

I found that articles posted online are really helpful. Somebody will say this is one specific technique that I'm doing right now, or this worked for me. Those kinds of things are more helpful because they typically are more big picture. So when I know what I need then, I'll try to look it up and try to find somebody who's written about it. Otherwise, I tend to do trial and error.

*Do you outline? Or do you just write?*

**JAC:** I used to be a very dedicated write by the seat of my pants writer. But I really have found that I go down the rabbit hole. I've learned to outline. I didn't with *The Wicked and the Just*, but the one I just finished had a month-by-month structural outline because I found that if I didn't plan it out, I didn't know what I was doing.

But again, that's learn to write this book stuff. I said "I will never outline, it is too restrictive." But then this book came along and I had to throw that out the window and make an outline because it's what the book needs. So going forward I'm going to try to be more of an outliner, even though my outlines are often very, very high concept.

They're often one sentence, this happens and then that happens. But the one I did for the book I just finished was just ridiculous. It was color coded. The emotional arc was pink and all that, because it wasn't coming together in my head. It needed that, it really did.

*Sometimes it can be really hard to kind of break out of those grand proclamations that you've made about how this is how I write, and do something different. So I love that you're able to do that.*

**JAC:** I have to. You can't be static. Writing is such a dynamic thing because every book that you write changes you a little bit. It's like growing up. You have these experiences and they each make you a different person as you become an adult. So if you disregard those lessons, why suffer through them if you're not going to learn anything?

*What do you like about the Pacific Northwest? What keeps you here?*

**JAC:** I grew up in Spokane, so I'm from here. I lived in New Jersey for six years and it was, it was a good experience. It was educational. It really reminded me that this country's really big and it feels like a foreign country in some places. The value system is so different. I had to even adjust my vocabulary. I remember getting there and telling people I'm from Washington. They'd say, "Oh, the capital. I really like it there." And I had to remind them that the world doesn't end at the Alleghenies.

I'm glad I had that experience, but I was very happy to come back. Mainly what keeps me here is the vibe of the place. With the tech companies here, we just have this creative energy. They're people who want to create things for a living. You have Nintendo. You have Steam. You have Wizards of the Coast. You've got Microsoft. They're all people who have made a living making things from nothing. And writers and artists fit into that community because they want to do the same thing, just with a different medium. So I really like the optimism, this upbeat tone of the place. The coffee is really good. There are a lot of things to recommend it. It's close to the water. The climate's real nice. It's got a very dynamic sort of characteristic to it that I really like, and I would be hard pressed to leave again.

*Do you think that there's something about the Pacific Northwest that has kind of led to all this creativity? Or just all this creativity has made the Pacific Northwest what it is? The chicken or the egg?*

**JAC:** Part of what has made this part of the world this way is its history. It's got a homesteading type of roots. It's drawn a certain kind of person over the years. First it was Homestead Act, then it was the rail terminus. It was the gold rush and Seattle was the jumping off point for the Alaska gold rush. So it's drawn people here who are willing to take a risk. They're willing to try something new. They're willing to go to a whole new place, around new people and learn something. Whether that's how to cut down big trees, that's how to run a tugboat, that's going to the gold fields. It's that kind of restlessness almost that's brought people.

The people that are back east, and you can really tell, they are a sort of a piece. The way that people on the west coast are of a sort of a piece. Not that it's good or bad, it's just different. I think that's why I had a hard time fitting in back there—I didn't understand it. And it took me a long time to really recognize that it was just a different way to think about the world.

*That is true. It's so easy to leave in this day and age. It's not like it used to be where it would take you however long to ride the train to the other part of the country.*

**JAC:** And it was expensive, too. Typically one way.

*How do you connect with other writers here and outside of the area?*

**JAC:** Well, most of my connections with other writers have been over the Internet. When *The Wicked and The Just* sold, it was just 2010, and the first thing I did was join online sort of support groups for people whose first books for kids were going to come out in 2012. That was the best thing I did because it put me in contact with other people who were right at the same point in their careers as I was. So nobody really felt out of their depth. We were all worried about copy edits at the same time. We were all worried about cover reveals and reviews. It was all happening over the space of a year, but it was still the same set of experiences. It's been really good.

We still keep in touch. So I'm still talking to these people. A lot of them live in the area, so we get together for coffee. We have holiday parties and meet for drinks. So that's really nice, too. I didn't really hang out with other writers before I had my book deal because I felt like a huge imposter. I had that problem, and I shouldn't have.

*What is that about we writers that we're always like so afraid someone's going to look behind the curtain and find the truth?*

**JAC:** A lot of what we do is so much bravado. We have a lot of hubris to think that we can write something that other people will want to read and pay money for. So we're all pretty sure we're imposters. If we're being honest, I don't think any of us would say otherwise. But I also hang out with people from my agency. There are 12 of us in the area. It's good to have somebody around who understands. I mean my husband is great and he is super supportive but I remember very specifically when I got my starred review from Kirkus. When my editor told me, and I ran and told my husband, "Yay! Kirkus gave me a star. I got a starred review." He replied, "Yay! What's Kirkus?" Other writers kind of get that because Kirkus will savage you. They savage everybody. So when they like you that's a big deal. So having those people around who understand it and get it, is, it's invaluable. I'm sorry I didn't do it sooner.

*What do you think held you back?*

**JAC:** Total imposter syndrome. When I had tried to do in-person critique groups in the past, I found them to be very mismatched. It's usually just that you're at a different point in your writing than the other people in the group, or it just doesn't gel for whatever reason. It made me kind of leery of that kind of thing. I also would feel very uncomfortable hanging out with writers who had 20 books under their belt. I would definitely feel like an imposter there. Hanging out with other writers who have one or two books, it's the right speed.

*If critique groups don't work, where do you look for feedback?*

**JAC:** Before I had my book deal, I found beta readers through my LiveJournal. I've kept a LiveJournal since about 2003. Mostly it was other writers that I hung out with and chatted with and eventually we just started trading manuscripts. Some of them worked and some of them didn't, but there's been two that have really connected and their feedback is the kind of feedback that's helpful to me.

It's been interesting to get different kinds of feedback over the years, and I've really kind of been able to figure out what's useful and what's not in a hurry. Now I'm very fortunate to have my agent and my editor giving me feedback. So I've got the feedback from my beta readers, which is more from a reader point of view, and then from my agent and my editor, which is very much more of a professional sales and marketing, here's what the market's doing kind of feedback. But it's also very nuanced. Feedback like, "I don't feel like this character would do this." "Why is this happening because two pages ago you said this?" "You used the word grey three times in this paragraph." That kind of thing.

I've been very fortunate in that I've managed to figure out which people give the best feedback for me. And they've been very tolerant to read all my stuff again and again and continue to offer me really good feedback.

*How much weight do you give to the feedback that you get from these people? I know that you trust them, that's why you keep going to them. Do you have times when you're like, "you know I really appreciate that but ..."*

**JAC:** Typically, I don't give chapter by chapter, I've not had to do that yet. I'm sure I will have to someday but typically I've just turned over a whole manuscript. So usually, when I get the feedback sent back to me, I will try to carve out as much time as possible to just read it all in context—the manuscript and the feedback.

Typically as I'm reading it, it shapes into three basic categories. The first is yeah that was wrong, I'm definitely going to fix that. And then there's, well I kind of see where you're going with this but I don't necessarily agree with the suggestion so it needs more thought. And rarely there'll be no, that stays and here's why. I don't have those very often anymore. And if I ever have one that's really a strong reaction, that always gives me pause because that's a darling I might need to murder. It's a little bit too precious. But there have been times when I have kind of drawn those lines.

But usually, I'm very fortunate that the feedback I get is less here's a suggestion and it's more, this doesn't work for me. And I guess here's an example: I recently turned in a manuscript to my agent and she read it and gave feedback. On the first scene she said to me, "Too much is happening in this scene, I got confused." And I sat there, I had probably rewritten this scene 12 times already. So I sat and took it apart and said okay what is this scene trying to do? I diced it down to the four different points that I want the story to pivot on for the rest of the book. Can any of them be moved to the next scene? I took the scene and rewrote it, moving some of the action to the next scene. That change had the additional advantage of focusing everything onto the main character, which I kind of realized is where she was going with it. The idea that she was confused. After I trimmed everything down and refocused this scene, it let me solve the problem that she pointed out but also kind of enhanced the scene again. And she really liked it and thought it was funny. So it turned out that was the right thing to do.

That's how I try to approach feedback. I think about what I'm trying to do and whether I'm achieving it. Because if somebody is pointing out to me that it's not working, I'm clearly not achieving it. So I need to figure out how to fix it. I'm very fortunate that my beta readers and my agent and my editor are always hesitant to tell me how. They are usually much more interested in telling me, "This is not working. It's your job, you're the writer, you fix it."

*Are your beta readers part of your flock of readers in general? Would they read you after you're published?*

**JAC:** I know one of them does. She's a teacher and she's always talking about how she would like to, she talks it up to her fellow teachers. The other beta reader, I don't know. I guess. We just trade manuscripts. I think she has read it, but I'm not sure.

*So how do you connect with your readers?*

**JAC:** I spend way too much time on Twitter.

*As do we all. That is the drawback of Twitter.*

**JAC:** When you're writing for young adults, it's really weird. Because they don't like things that are too weird. So being in their space is weird. If you're going to be in their space, you have to be awesome in some way. You have to make them laugh. You have to make them think. You have to bring something to the table, because they have a lot to do in their lives. They have homework. They've got clubs. They've got dark poetry of their own to write.

If I was a little awesomer, I would probably go on YouTube, because I do know that that is where my readers hang out. But I am not photogenic, and I'm not that interesting. So I don't know that I would be successful on YouTube. I know that really works for some people because they have a stage presence and they can, you know, be funny and silly and they do whatever they do. But I don't think that's me. I work on trying to be authentic. Kids respond to that. They really respond to adults who don't try too hard, but who also kind of have a good sense of where the boundaries are. They don't try to be a kid themselves. They're a cool adult who isn't lame.

I do Tumblr now, too. But mostly the people who I talk to on Twitter and Tumblr are librarians and teachers. I count on them to be the ones to slide my book across the table to them and say, here, try this. Because I have the kind of book that kids are made to read and often end up liking anyway.

*So, what do you think about the book that you have finished now? Do you think that it will be in that same vein? Where it's what you have to read and then you end up liking it?*

**JAC:** It's very much the kind that kids will be made to read and hopefully will end up liking. It's hard because once you have a book published your job is to, I don't want to say build a brand but more like a readership. I was nudged towards this idea and told, look after a couple of books you can write something else. This is a good decision career wise. It's just been tricky to try to bottle lightning twice.

*Yeah, it's interesting the interplay between the creativity and the market forces.*

**JAC:** Often, I find it to be kind of arbitrary and random. I'm never sure at what point the market is really doing what it's doing and at what point it's being manipulated. It's like the gods are fighting, and I'm down here on the ground. I'm a mortal, so I don't have any control over that. So I write books—that's what I can do.

"Trust the process, and don't get too wrapped up in structure and in making sure that you're following somebody else's directives. Do what the book needs."

— *J. Anderson Coats*

# 4 Sage Cohen

Sage Cohen is the author of *The Productive Writer: Tips & Tools to Help You Write More, Stress Less & Create Success*; *Writing the Life Poetic: An Invitation to Read and Write Poetry*; and the poetry collection *Like the Heart, the World*. Her essay "The Word is the Way" appeared alongside thought leaders such as Barack Obama, Al Gore, and Thomas L. Friedman in the anthology *How to Achieve a Heaven on Earth*. Her poetry has been published widely in journals including: *Poetry Flash, The San Francisco Reader, La Petite Zine, Comet,* and *Mudfish*. She has won first prize in the Ghost Road Press poetry contest and been nominated for a Pushcart Prize. She lectures and teaches widely (including a range of interactive, online classes) and publishes the *Writing the Life Poetic Zine*.

Sage received her BA in Comparative Literature at Brown University and her MA in English, Creative Writing from New York University. She has taught creative writing to university students and led a writing program for patients in a residential hospital.

---

*One of the things that I think is really interesting about poetry is just how concise and tight it needs to be. And so I'm wondering what you do to get to where you need to be on that brevity.*

**Sage Cohen:** Yes, this kind of brevity in poetry is called compression. Often our work involves distilling ideas or experiences to an image or a phrase with attention to the music of the language. For me, one of the most interesting opportunities of poetry is using language to give people a visceral experience. I've been obsessed with making poems since about age 14. So this relationship between compression and experience is a problem I've been wanting to solve my whole life. It fascinates me. I'm always trying to invite the reader to land in the essence of something.

A useful revision strategy in poetry is to find the "scaffolding" of a poem. Often there is an expository stanza or two at the beginning or end that detracts from the poem and can be pared down. I often write into a poem and discover through the writing what is the most essential part and what can be carved away. The more ruthless I am in my attention compression, the easier it is to see what needs to be opened up and investigated more.

*Sometimes when you're writing a short story or something, you just cut out the first five pages because you realize once you've gotten through it, oh, this is where it really starts. So is that kind of the same thing?*

**SC:** Yes! It's often very similar in poetry. You write to find your way in, and you think it's going to be a poem about a blackbird, but it's actually about your mother's black shoes, and then you discover it's about the funeral where she wore those shoes when you were eight-years old. William Stafford calls this following the golden thread, letting the poem lead you someplace. And that's what I love about the writing life, period. No matter what you're writing, you're just following and trusting the words or the images that you're in pursuit of. The place where we end up can be quite unexpected.

*Have you ever had anything that just came out exactly the way you wanted it to on the first run?*

**SC:** I've had a handful of poems that seemed to just arrive. And they felt cut from whole cloth. I once heard Tess Gallagher speak about a book of hers, I think it was *Moon Crossing Bridge*. She said that she felt most of the poems in that collection were given to her, and that it was incredibly difficult to write after that because receiving poems and writing poems are two very different experiences. You have to be careful when the poems arrive not to expect that other poems will come to you in the same way. I consider everything I write to be a kind of weightlifting or training. I'm readying myself to be receptive. I'm training myself to gather up what is moving through and available to me. My writing practice has always felt like I am cultivating the channel through which poems are glimpsed.

*Do you have any special processes or rituals that you go through to make that happen when you need it to?*

**SC:** For many years, I started with free writing. My day job as a marketing consultant involves strategic thinking and copywriting. So, the free writing got me into a looser and more receptive state of mind. I would have words coming without planning them. And it was a really interesting way to see the images, themes, and language that were moving through me. Things would just come and surprise me. At this stage, that process of discovery has become baked in. I can just sit down and go. I'll get an image or an interesting phrase on a dog walk or at work and I'll move immediately into the mode of poem creation. I think it's because I have all that free writing anchored in my nervous system. I can get free quickly now. I don't have to labor to unburden myself as much.

*It's kind of like an actor's sense memory. Like you just do something enough that it becomes so natural.*

**SC:** Yes! It's like scales. I did my free writing scales forever. Now my fingers know how to do them. That doesn't guarantee I'll be a concert pianist. It just means I know my scales. This makes the labors of creation less effortful and more joyful

*When you and I have talked before, you mentioned that if ideas for poetry come to you while you're in the middle of doing that copywriting, that you capture them and come back to them when the time is right. Have*

*you ever had problems like getting back into where that came from?*

**SC:** It's not really one of my problems, fortunately. I have the luxury of working for myself, which a lot of times is a luxury, which gives me the flexibility to write down whatever comes, wherever I am, whatever it is. If I'm at my desk doing client work and a poem presents itself, sometimes I just pause for 10 minutes and really follow it where the language leads me, and then put it aside to complete later. I can usually move back and forth pretty easily between poems and business copy. I've spent nearly 20 years experimenting with what's the right time for what kind of work, and I think this is an important distinction for every writer to figure out on their own.

*Definitely.*

**SC:** I think I finally learned it's too hard to make myself do what I'm resisting doing—within reason, of course! If I've got a poem through, the most efficient thing to do may be just to write that poem for a little bit, and then when I get back to whatever the other work is, I'm really kind of invigorated. So, that's something I've never stopped experimenting with—how to honor the energy of what wants to come through. I can do this because I know that I'm reliable to myself and my clients. I always meet my deadlines. So in that context, I feel freer to dedicate myself to whatever needs to happen right now to make the best use of me as a writing vessel.

*Because you could spend the next four hours just trying to push that back and then not being effective of what you have decided I have to do right now.*

**SC:** And being distracted by it. Instead, I focus on how they cross-fertilize. When I'm really engaged with whatever it is, writing a brochure for a client or a website copy, it spills over and it makes me feel excited about the poetry, or if I really let myself have that 10 minutes or half hour of the poem, it feeds others. I look at it as an ecosystem where any writing I do maximizes my impact in all of the other writing I do rather than looking at it as one taking from the other.

*Right. You know, and that was actually one of the questions that I was hoping to ask you today, was how do you think that copywriting has made you a better poet? And then, of course, vice versa, how does poetry help with your copywriting?*

**SC:** I know there are writers who feel like one robs from the other. That has never been my experience. I am so satisfied if I am solving a problem in writing, and copywriting and poetry are just different sets of problems. The compression of poetry translates really well to finding the nut of the story in copywriting. And having an ear for sound can make headlines sing. Knowing how to manipulate emotion with language, and being able to present an image that's tangible and intentional is very useful in copywriting. So poetry has been very valuable for my copywriting.

Plus, copywriting gives me 8-12 hours a day of writing practice, so I never lose my chops while supporting my family. Getting paid is a great way of reinforcing a writing practice! Over the years of copywriting, I've become a better thinker about how to use language, and there's no endpoint; It's just a constant evolution of learning, which really satisfies me.

A poem is more of a discovery process. Copywriting is also somewhat of a discovery process, but the destination has already been determined. What I like about poems is that, in some ways, they're in charge. I feel like I'm just following them around picking up their little petals, trying to put the flower back together. I really appreciate that the different types of writing move in different ways. I think for me, variety is key. I would not want to sit around and write poems all day. I'm more of a generalist that way. I write poetry. I write essays. I write how-to books. I write marketing copy. And for me, that sort of constellation keeps me fresh.

*I don't know if you've ever done a strengths finder. I did one of those not too long ago, and one of my strengths was learner. I'm starting to think that most writers have learning as one of their strengths and their passions. I'm just wondering if you feel like you're a learner in life because you're writing, or that writing serves your learning.*

**SC:** It's almost like a chicken/egg thing. I mean I love that my career is so hard.  I'm going to die still trying to become the best writer I can be. It's not something you ever arrive at. I remember after I wrote my first how-to book, I thought, well, now I know how to write a how-to book so the next one should be pretty easy, right? Nope. I figured out how to write one how-to book, and then the next how-to book had to be figured out all over again. It's just endlessly satisfying discovering how each piece of writing wants to be shaped and presented. That dance of receiving and steering and witnessing is always a revelation. I am endlessly amazed by the alchemy of taking experience in and putting words back out and trying to discover where the writing needs to go. So yes, that's a very long answer. Yes. I am grateful to be a student of writing. It's a powerful partner dance. I'm always exploring when to lead and when to follow.

There's a Flannery O'Conner quote that says, "I write because I don't know what I think until I read what I say." There's a way that writing is a way of witnessing myself and being in conversation with myself that makes it hard for me to relate to people who feel lonely.

So there's a feeling of like communing with myself through whatever I'm writing that has been such a powerful, not even life skill, but life's gift to me. And I've always hoped that people who aren't attracted to writing have some other way of communicating with themselves and making sense of . . .

*Whatever is around us?*

**SC:** Yeah. This crazy thing called life.

*What do you love reading the most? What gets you the most passionate?*

**SC:** I love *Sun Magazine*. I love reading poetry. I love reading fiction. I love reading how-to books. If there's something with personal development I'm working on, I'll go find a book on that. So at any given time I'm reading several different kinds of books that range from what inspires me, what entertains me, what helps me learn. When I read, I'm always studying what writers are doing with their craft.

*Can you think of any book or other piece that really just got you inspired to do something amazing?*

**SC:** When I read Lidia Yuknavich's memoir *The Chronology of Water*, it kind of threw the doors open for me. Reading it felt like drowning. I was so immersed, and then at the end I took this big gasp and was amazed to still be alive. I read it at a time when my own life was pretty difficult, and that story was embodied in a way that I was hungry for—that is so important and so rare in writing. I was intrigued by how she created so much tension about an event that was never named but still had so much power.

I was also humbled by Ariel Gore's *The End of Eve*. I have a memoir project of my own that I am starting to circle. So I am studying how we tell these kind of epic stories and tease out what it is that needs to be told.

*I wanted to talk to you about the Pacific Northwest and what inspiration you get from living here.*

**SC:** Being able to hike in the rainforest is huge for me, for my writing, for my heart. It's just so powerful. And for the most part I have found the rain to be really cozy and writerly. I get my cup of tea and enjoy that it's wet out there and not in here. It's much less distracting than sunshine. When it's sunny it's really hard to sit in my chair.

I had no idea when I moved to Portland what a rich literary community this is. I am constantly amazed and grateful for the quality of human beings, the incredible writers and incredible people in every square inch of this city. And there are so many different communities of writers, so many opportunities to attend readings, events, and conferences. This makes it a very, very lush place.

*A lot of the people I've talked to have said that the weather is the reason there are so many writers because what the heck else are we going to do?*

**SC:** Yeah.

*We just sit inside and type away.*

**SC:** Pet our cats or write.

*Or do both at the same time. I don't currently have any cats but all of the cats I've had, the second you sit down at the computer, they're like, 'Oh, I need to come sit down on your lap now.'*

**SC:** Yes! My cat Diablo kind of drapes himself over my arms so I'm typing and I'm holding 10 pounds up also, which maybe is good exercise, or maybe it's just killing my arms.

He wants to be a part of it.

*Yeah. I think that's the deal with cats is that they always want to see what's going on. They don't always want to be part of it. They just want to be aware.*

**SC:** Right. They want to feel like they have some say.

*So, if an aspiring writer came up to you and said, "Hey, what's the one thing that I need to do to be better at this writing thing?" What would you say?*

**SC:** Keep writing. Write as much as you can and stay connected to what you love about writing. Do whatever you can to keep that love alive, that courtship going. There are endless ways to do that, and it's going to be different for everybody. Taking classes for some people can be very useful in terms of having structure and having accountability, and learning about craft from people that you admire. Find a community. It could be just one other person, but having that feedback loop of other people who care about what you care about can be so powerfully affirming and energizing. I have one friend who sends me short stories she loves. And I'll read them and we'll have an email conversation. Having a friend who is as thrilled by the way a writer constructs a sentence as I am makes me feel like I belong on this earth. It keeps me going.

*What is your advice to someone who is afraid to not take that feedback from someone that they admire or who feels like it's just not right for what they're trying to do?*

**SC:** Increase your exposure. That's it. The most valuable thing that I got out of my MFA experience was learning that you put 12 people in a room and there are going to be 12 different opinions about what to do with your poem. Including the three famous poets who were teaching. They all are going to tell you completely different things about your poems.

Your job as a writer is to learn who your teachers are and who your peers are that are truly useful to you. So, if you're getting information that doesn't feel right, go reality test it. Take another class with another teacher. If you have 10 teachers who have all told you the same exact thing, you might want to seriously reconsider your position. It's so easy to think that there's only one right way or we have to change something because some person we admire told us to. But the agonizing truth about writing is that we are our only expert. We take in feedback, and then it's our job to decide what feedback is serving us.

Be willing to experiment and have fun with it, but focus on training your ear. We're training our ear for language, but we're also training our ear for what guidance makes sense and what guidance doesn't and tracking over time who are the right kind of teachers. Just like not everyone's the right partner for us. Not everyone's the right therapist for us. Not everyone's the right teacher for us.

*Have you ever had a time when someone who was a teacher or when a friend of yours gave you that one thing that had been holding you back on a piece?*

**SC:** Like help me crack the code of it?

*Yes, and you're like, "Yes. That's what I've been trying to get at."*

**SC:** Not exactly. But here's an example of how I tried to set myself up for that kind of experience. I have a memoir that I am intending to write, and I took a storytelling class where the goal was to perform a story that you have never written down in front of a live audience. I thought that speaking the story first might give me a fresh way in to discovering what the organizing principle and key themes might be.

It was so interesting approaching a story without writing it down, just seeing what story presented itself. And I did not end up figuring out the memoir in that class. I came up with a different related story. But then a month later the nutshell of the memoir came through in an essay that I wrote in an hour. So it wasn't so much another person helping me, but me putting myself in a context where I didn't really know what I was doing. Putting myself into a beginner's mind helped me eventually identify and shape the story. The struggle to get it sorted out within the five weeks of the class was extremely valuable—even though I didn't meet the goal.

The journey was more of a scenic route than I expected, but I eventually arrived at my destination. As we write, we are always discovering when to push and when to let things present themselves. That's another dance that we spend our whole lives figuring out and never solve, but we're always dancing.

"No matter what you're
writing, you're just following
and trusting the words or the
images that you're in pursuit
of. The place where we end
up can be quite unexpected."

— *Sage Cohen*

# 5 Cricket Daniel

Playwright Cricket Daniel lives in Bend, Oregon but hails from California. Cricket holds a theater degree from UC Santa Barbara and studied Shakespeare in Cambridge, England. She has an extensive background in improv, stand-up, and theater. Cricket was a member of the national improv troupe Comedy Sportz, and performed stand-up at The Ice House and The Improv.

Cricket regularly performed in local community theatre productions. However, it was when she was an audience member one evening at a local production that she found her true calling. She happened to be in the audience watching a play the same night as the playwright and ended up watching him more than the play. By the end of the evening she thought to herself "I wanna be that guy!" The next day she started writing her first play. She has since had plays produced across the country.

---

*What brought you to the northwest?*

**Cricket Daniel:**
My husband and I moved to Bend, Oregon from Santa Barbara 19 years ago. My husband was born and raised in Colorado, so this felt like home to him. I have been freezing for 19 years, but I do love it here and it is a wonderful place to raise our 10-year-old daughter. It wasn't until I became a stay-at-home-mom that I started writing plays, and then I found success in that, and I have not looked back. I definitely found my niche.

*Did you intend to become a writer when you moved to Oregon?*

**CD:** My background was in stand-up, and in comedy, and improv. I think I secretly always knew I was a writer. My degree from Santa Barbara is a theater degree with an emphasis in writing, but I was such a fame whore. I wanted to be on stage in front of the camera in the lights, always. I guess I've matured a lot, because that is not the case anymore, but when we moved here 19 years ago, it was basically for portability.

*How does the process work there in Bend? Do you have a lot of local theatres that you can work with to produce?*

**CD:** No. I have worked out of one theatre. I'm the resident playwright out of 2nd Street Theatre, and Maralyn Thoma, who used to write for soap operas for years and years, owns it. We actually moved to Bend the exact same time, and we ended up being in a play together at one of the theatres. Fast-forward to a few years later, she opened up her own theatre.

Bend has a lot of theatre—really great stuff. So when I wrote my first play and it came hot off the presses, I thought, oh my god, they're going to be fighting over this, right? Wrong! I took it to the two theaters in Bend at that time, including 2nd Street Theater. I learned very quickly that theaters and their seasons are dictated by two things—directors and audiences. Directors like to direct plays that they have a connection to or have a passion for. Audiences like to see plays that they have heard of or are well known. I couldn't get anyone in Bend to take a chance on it.

And here I am with this great play that I'm convinced is the funniest thing I've ever seen or read. So I started sending out queries to only Oregon theatres. Thank goodness Jason Icenbice in Klamath Falls took a chance on me. He fought really hard for me and for *Couple Dating*, my first play. I will be forever grateful for him.

*Couple Dating*, made its world premier in Klamath Falls at a little playhouse called the Linkville Playhouse. Klamath Falls has some wonderful actors there. My family, friends, and I all traveled to Klamath Falls in November 2009, and we saw *Couple Dating* on stage for the first time. Talk about a high. That was better than any audience applause as an actress on stage ever. After Maralyn saw it, she says, "This has to come to Bend," and I said, "I know." I got the best director in town, and *Couple Dating* made its debut in Bend the following year, 2010, and I have produced one play a year at 2nd Street Theatre ever since.

*Wow. So what is it like giving your play up to a director?*

**CD:** You know, it's easy when I'm working with a director of my choice. Susan Benson is my director in Bend. I trust and respect her. She actually makes my plays better. I always say, I give her a paint-by-numbers, and she adds all the color. We have a great relationship. I have seen my plays produced in other theaters where I was like, oh my gosh, I wish I had more of a hand in it. It's kind of hard, but you have to get used to it.

Just yesterday I had a play produced in Eugene, and I didn't have a chance to see it. There are times when my plays are going to be on stage, and I have no say at all. You just hope that they get the intention behind the words, and they'll always have a different perspective.

That's what I kind of like. When I write my plays, I don't put in a whole lot of blocking or direction because I know every director's going to come in with their own vision, and I respect that. The only thing I don't want them doing is changing my words without asking me.

I have been approached by theatres before where they said, "We have an actress who's not really comfortable with those lines. Would you be willing to tweak them?" Absolutely. If it gets produced on your stage, I'm willing to tweak some lines. Absolutely. I'm a very accommodating writer, as long as they run it by me first. It's simple to hand it over when I work with Susan. We're a team. I've seen productions of mine where it's not exactly the way I would've done, and I've seen it another way that I probably have grown to love, but hey, if the check's in the mail, and it's one more stage I can put on my website saying, "My play's been produced," because I'm telling you, I'm not published yet, and that's the next goal. I have to be patient. That will come. Right now, I'm just trying to get my plays on as many stages as I can. Once they have been produced in a big market with real reviews, I hope that they will get published. Once published, the productions will hopefully get easier and more of them. Right now, getting theaters to take a chance on a new play by an unknown playwright is difficult. Theaters like to go with the tried and true.

I always say it's a lot like when you go to the grocery store and you see two products. They're identical. One's $3.98. One's $2.98. You tend to go with the $3.98 because it must be better. Why is it a dollar more? And so they're looking at these plays and like, "God, we really like Cricket Daniel's plays. She's out of Oregon, but it's only been produced one or two times, and our audiences have never heard of it, and they tend to like to go with what they've heard about or have seen before," and so, a lot of times a theatre will love my stuff and ultimately not pick it.

*What do you think was the key with the Klamath Falls theatre?*

**CD:** You know, it just resonated with Jason Icenbice, and I thank him in every single program. And any time I have the liberty of being on stage to say hello to my audiences and thank them for being there, I give him a shout out. He was the first producer who truly took a chance on me, and he literally had to haggle the hell out of it to get it put on. And you know what? *Couple Dating* grossed more money that season than any other play, because it was hysterical and it caused some controversy.

I tend to touch on subjects that most people don't want to touch, and I try to put a funny spin on topics that are usually controversial and hot button topics, but Jason Icenbice took a chance on me and that play. He loved it right out of the gate, and I didn't get paid a lot of money for it, and he liked the idea that I would be there opening night. He liked the idea of having it as a world premier, and he just took a chance, and he honestly took a big chance. I think he had to give up one play that he wanted to do in place of mine. He just had to do a whole little, you know, trading up for me, and I'll always, always be thankful to him.

*That is really amazing.*

**CD:** Because once you're able to say in your query, "I am a produced playwright," rather than, "I am a new playwright. Will you take a chance on someone like me? I've got this play. I think it's funny. At least read it." Once you put produced in front of you, a lot more doors open, and so, thanks to Jason Icenbice, a lot more doors opened.

*That sounds like it was a really great fit with him. You did mention that you did stand-up comedy before you started writing. What do you think you learned from doing that that's really helped you be funny in your plays?*

**CD:** I think I learned a lot about the setup of a joke because, as a stand-up, you're writing your own material, and it's a lot of a one-two punch. When you see my plays, you feel like this girl clearly comes from a background of stand-up and wants to be a sitcom writer. You almost feel like there should be a laugh track. The scenarios are very sitcom-y. They are so funny, and for two hours, you're going to laugh your butt off.

I'm not trained as a playwright. When people say, "Oh, by this page, you should be introducing the protagonist, and the arc, and blah blah blah," I just spew out what I think is funny. I tighten it up. I go through it again, and again, and again, and if an arc happens, great.

I'm not going out to write something that's going to change your life, although my last play, *Helen on Wheels*, is about an elderly lady who lost her husband. She's having a hard time moving on. I had two grown men leave the audience one night and approach me with tears in their eyes saying, "I lost my wife. I can't thank you enough for what this play meant for me. It just showed me that I can go on, and she would want me to go on and possibly even date again." I have seen people cry in my plays, and that is extraordinary, that feeling of sitting there watching them wipe away tears, and know "My play did that. My little old play, you know?" It's amazing.

*Do you find yourself getting caught up in the emotions when you're writing?*

**CD:** Everything I write, I have very much experienced. I write things that are very close to my heart. The characters I know. I'm usually one of them in a way. I'll make it pretty colorful and take liberties, but every single play of mine is my story, and I know these people, and so it does hit close to home. I've had a play that I consider very much a dedication to my father, who's no longer with me. That was all his stories. When you hear Sal Santoro going down memory lane, that's my dad. He thinks he invented the bagel and the Lender brothers stole the idea from him.

I mean, those were his stories, and so, when I see that, I'm like, this is for you, Dad, and my last one, *Helen on Wheels*, when she breaks out of jail—she got thrown in there for a bingo controversy—that's my mom.

My mother never got to see any of my plays, she passed away

before I started writing them, as did my father. So I love to kind of have them both be part of this by writing their stories and dedicating plays to them.

*Where do you feel like the words come from? Because you take your experiences, but then it goes beyond that.*

**CD:** It's so funny, because even my husband, he still can't believe this is happening, that I'm writing plays that are selling out and the people are laughing and crying. He'll say, "Did you write that?"
"Yes, sweetie, I wrote that."
"Yeah, but did you write that line?"
"Yes, I wrote all of that. I have it in me."

I always start with pretty much the play sketched out in my mind. I usually know how it starts. I know where it's going. I know how it ends. I usually have the title. I jot down hard copy. I will hand write all the characters, and what their names are, and what their idiosyncrasies are, and what their intent is, possibly, within the play. So when I sit down to write it, it's pretty clear in my head how it's going to go. The lines, literally, as I am typing them, I'll see sparks flying off my fingers because I don't know where they come from. Honestly, that's just I guess when you know you've got it, right? It shouldn't be so hard. They just come. The funny just comes.

I am a funny person. I think that helps. I've been funny my whole life. I was telling jokes and writing jokes right out of the womb. So it helps that it comes naturally.

What I am known for as a playwright is the banter. It's the give and take. It's the one-two punch between the two characters or the three characters. It's very rare on a page in one of my scripts that you've got chunks of dialogue. It's only when I go into the dramatic moments—and I have been known to do that, to take it down a notch, tug at the heartstrings—but most of my pages, if you were to look at them, one line, one line, one line, one word, one line.

Because the banter, the dialogue, I am able to write that very funny back and forth dialogue, and my plays are pretty...you can identify them pretty quickly. Outside of one play, they are always back east within the time. Catholic family at the heart of it all, and to me, Italians and people who live back east, they are hysterical. They can say things that nobody else can say and get away with it, and you find it charming. Only someone from back east can say, "I don't mean no disrespect, but your sister's a whore." No one else can say that, and it's funny, right?

*Did you spend any time back there?*

**CD:** No. But I know I was meant to be a Jersey Girl. There's no doubt in my mind, and people will...when they meet me, they'll say, "Where are you from, back east? I hear it in your voice." I'm like, "Oh, that's the biggest compliment you could ever give me. I'm not from back east." My entire family; however, my siblings and my parents, were all born in West Haven, Connecticut, which is the setting of my second play, *Love, Laughter & Lucci*, but I was the only kid born and raised in California, and I've not spent a lot of time back east, and I set my plays in places where I've never been. *Helen on Wheels* was set in Oklahoma. Never been there. *Couple Dating* is set in Brooklyn. Never been there, but I just feel like I know these people.

*One of the things that I think is actually really interesting about plays is that you can do so much with so few characters. It's almost like poetry, where you really take it down to the bone.*

**CD:** Yeah. *Couple Dating* has like, eight. Four was the lowest I've ever had. Five to eight is what I normally have because I like the mayhem that comes in with a bunch of other characters—*Love, Laughter & Lucci*, there was just no call for it.

I also try to keep my plays simple, because I know if it calls for people flying in from the rafters and special effects, they're not going to produce my play. I need to make them as simple as they can get. They're usually set in a home with a kitchen and a living room. I don't have them going on a bunch of locations because I just know that a theatre is not going to want to produce it. They're going to say, "We don't have the wing space. We don't have the room. We don't have the budget."

So I try to keep my plays pretty stripped down where it's all about the dialogue. It's all about these people who you just love. They're all adorable.

I am a fairly predictable writer. At the end, I want the dreams to come true. I want the little bow on top. So at the end of *Love, Laughter & Lucci*, yeah, she gets the call from *All My Children*. I would've been pissed if she didn't. I write as an audience member. I know what I like, and when I go to a movie or I go to a play, if *All My Children* hadn't called, I would've been like, "I can't believe *All My Children* didn't call. I am so upset right now."

I write very endearing characters that are funny, that are relatable. I don't care who you are, when you see my plays, there's somebody who you're like, "Oh my gosh, I know that person," or "That person is me." I love doing that for people. That's why we watch the shows we watch because we can identify. So I don't want to write a play that I've not lived or know, and I don't want to write a play that people can't relate to. I want it to be a tuna casserole. You want to go out for your little lamb chop and fancy drizzle all over the plate? Go ahead. When you come to my plays, you're having tuna casserole, and who doesn't love a good casserole?

*It is. It's very comforting.*

**CD:** Yes. My plays are casseroles. I want you leaving full and feeling good about yourself, and yummy, and happy.

*How have you made the transition from being on stage to being behind the scenes?*

**CD:** I've turned into a chicken. I don't have it in me anymore. I like being in the background watching everybody and letting my actors get all the applause, because they deserve it. I mean, I write the words, but you know, what they do with it and the director, I want them to get all, all of the acclaim. I don't see myself being on stage anymore.

I used to always want to be on stage, and when I became a stay-at-home mom, I couldn't be in plays anymore, because it's a two-month commitment. I had a baby at home, and so I couldn't be gone every night for rehearsal and then gone every night for performances. But my husband and I would still attend the plays locally, and every single play we would attend, he would turn to me and say, "You wish you were in this play, don't you?" And I'm like, "Well, God, what a great story, and the actors are so great. I would've loved to work with this director. So, yes, I would've loved to have been part of this play. I mean, it's killing me."

Then we went to a play at 2nd Street Theatre, *Garden Politics*. The writer, Michael Slade, he was in town to see it. And I have to say, that was the first play where I didn't want to be in it. I watched him the entire time in that director's chair, and I remember thinking, "I want to be that guy." The next day, I literally sat down on my couch and said, "I'm going to write a play," and on that Saturday, I sketched out scenarios I thought resonated to me in my life. On Sunday, I started writing *Couple Dating*, and I was done two weeks later.

*That's amazing.*

**CD:** It came pouring out of me. And it's by far my favorite one because it's my first and, I think, my funniest one. A lot of people are saying *Helen on Wheels* is the best one to date for me. It had the most layers to it. Everyone says we can tell you've grown as a playwright from *Helen*, but *Couple Dating* will always be my favorite one.

*I always wonder if people would react differently knowing that you were there. You know, they wouldn't laugh as loud.*

**CD:** Some people do. I'll see them reading the program, and my picture's always in it, and I'm sitting in the director's chair, which means I'm obviously somebody with the production. I had a lady after my last play say, "I noticed that you know all the words. Are you an understudy? Because I noticed you're mouthing all the words." I try not to do that, but I can't help it.

With *Helen on Wheels*, the two main characters are in their 70s, and the stories are so true, and real to life and how a 70-something woman would feel that people couldn't believe that I was the writer. I love that. It's like, how do you know these people? I was raised by these people. I was a change of life baby. My parents were older. They played bingo my entire life. My mom wore slacks all her life and rollers. But that's a big compliment when they can't believe I'm the writer.

*When you were sitting down to write that first play, what resources did you use to make sure that you were doing it right?*

**CD:** None. I wrote it on WordPerfect. I put the characters' names in the center all caps, and then I just wrote the dialogue underneath. I've had the sense to go back and redo *Couple Dating* because it was wrong, but it was good enough to get it read at least. But I had a feeling how a script should look. I had written a couple of scripts for *Seinfeld* and *Friends*, and I did take a playwriting course in college. At that point, it had been 20 years.

I've read enough scripts just being a wannabe sitcom writer. But if you were to go back and see the original *Couple Dating*, there are theaters that wouldn't get past the first two pages because of the formatting, I'm sure. I didn't have the correct font. I didn't have the blocking where it's supposed to be or the, "She sighs." That kind of stuff. I had it right in the middle of the dialogue. But it came pouring out of me so fast I didn't have a choice. I just had to get it out of me.

I've been in a writing group, and we'd go in circles. They would say, "The format is wrong, and they're going to throw it out." And I used to say, "I just think it's more important that the funny is on the page than formatting. I think they'll get past the fact that I didn't use size 12 Final Draft Courier New blah blah blah. If they find it funny enough, they'll look past that."

I've now since fine-tuned my formatting. I have Final Draft now, but *Couple Dating* was bare bones. It was guerilla theatre. Guerilla playwriting. I was just writing funny, and I knew it was funny. And then it was proved to be very funny in Klamath Falls. It was sold out.

*That's so great. How long did it run in Klamath Falls?*

**CD:** I'm looking at my poster now. It ran from November 6 to the 28. So a good three-week run.

I went to the audition. Boy, talk about when the playwright's in the audience. It throws the actors for a loop as well, not just the audience members. It freaks them out when the playwright shows up. They're not used to it. Most playwrights are dead. A lot of the community theatre productions, playwrights not going to just show up. So that's kind of weird, the dynamic. I went to go see a production in Colorado of mine, and it wasn't the best production I'd ever seen. I take that back, it was a wonderful production, but the nerves on the actors…it was opening night, and I was told it's because I was in the audience. It throws them for a loop, and I can see that, I suppose.

You know, those are your words, and you want to hit every single one perfect, and you don't. I now know I can't see my productions perfect. Some words are going to get dropped. Some lines are going to get dropped, and now I'm okay...and I was okay with it then, but you always hope for every funny joke to get in there. That's the cherry on top right there. That's the good stuff when you finally get to see it, right? It's fun. Actually, I saw a quote the other day, and it's so true: Being a writer is like having homework for the rest of your life, and it is, and I am a deadline writer.

If I don't have a deadline, I won't do it. I'm not the writer that says, I write from 8:00 to 10:00 every morning whether I have something to write to not. I just sit down and write. I don't do that. I do something every day. It's usually marketing myself. I usually submit to play festivals every day or a contest. I do something to get my name out there every single day, but unless I have a deadline, I'm not writing. I'm pretty bad that way.

*When you're going back and tweaking, what kinds of things are you fixing?*

**CD:** Usually I'll know when it's not funny on the page. I'll say, "Something's not right there," and so I think about it. I say it out loud. It's like punching up a script. You get some scriptwriters, and then you have people who actually come in and punch it up. I'll do all of that. I can hear if something falls flat and just needs to be funnier, or I'll tighten it. I tend to be too long. My directors say, "Cricket, you got to cut about two pages out of that. She's going on and on about how they met, and blah blah blah." I'm like, "You're right. Scratch, scratch."
For the most part, I'm typing it up, and I'm punching it up the whole time. You have got to have that hook at the end, that zinger. I'm a zinger kind of writer.

*Do you do it after sometimes you see it produced and you're like, "Oh, I thought that worked on the page, but once I see it live, I need to fix this."*

CD: You're always amazed what happens when you see it live. Sometimes they're laughing at places that you didn't even intend to be funny. That's weird, you know? I wrote one scene that was meant to be a sad moment, and they laughed. People said, "Well, it's because it's an uncomfortable moment. Sometimes you laugh." But sure, after I'm done seeing it, yeah, I'll go back and tweak it, but not a whole lot. If it's produced in Bend, I'm producing it, and I'm there every night during rehearsals, and we're tweaking up until the end. Not a whole lot. I don't like to do that to the actors. By the time they audition, it's usually 100 percent, but every once in a while, something doesn't work. And it was the same way with stand-up. If you did it 50 times on stage and you don't get a laugh, you've got to cut it whether you think it's funny or not. So, every once in a while, I'm like, "God, I can't believe I have to cut that line. That is so funny."

Of course, after you've been in rehearsal for a month or two, it's never funny. None of it's funny. I'm sick of it myself. But then you get an audience, and you're like, "Oh, thank God. It is funny." But you're always surprised. They always laugh when you didn't expect it to be funny, and they never laugh at the one joke that you thought was brilliant.

And every audience is different. Friday night audiences are hard. They've been working all day. They're tired. Matinee audiences are great, believe it or not. Sometimes I'll say, "God, this audience is so quiet. They're giving my actors nothing." It's stressful to me, as a producer, sitting there. So during intermission, I'll say, "You guys are so quiet." "Really? We're laughing our asses off. We think it's the funniest thing we've ever seen." I'm like, "Okay, we're not hearing you. So feel free to chuckle out loud because my actors need something to work off of." It's weird sitting there as the writer watching the audience.

*Going back to your experience in stand-up, and I was thinking that must've really helped develop a really thick skin, because that's a rough business.*

**CD:** I had a standing gig every single week in downtown Santa Barbara. You get those people front row, "Make me laugh. I bet you can't make me laugh. Watch me stay here and not laugh." And you get people who think you suck—and they'll tell you. You get a thick skin real quick.

*Rejection is never easy, of course, but that must help you develop the attitude where it rolls off your back.*

**CD:** You can't let it affect you. I'm not saying it doesn't hurt. But you still have to keep writing more funny. You just chalk it up as "I'm not their cup of tea."

*Do you have any other advice for someone who's new to playwriting?*

**CD:** It's an old saying, but truly, you want to write what you know. Write about the scenarios in your life that are funny. Write about those memories that you have. Write about your wacky siblings, all your friends. Have fun, and let it pour out. Don't be confined by the rules of playwriting. Just write it all out and then tighten it up, and then maybe go back and format it and try to throw in some arcs or structure.

If you want to write a play, write about a situation that is either heart wrenching, funny, exciting, dramatic, mysterious—something you know, something that truly did happen. Write those characters. If you can get it to 89 to 110 pages, you're golden, baby. And you know what? At the end of the day, if you don't get it produced, at least you got one under your belt. The next one comes easier, and it's very rewarding. Eventually invest in yourself. Get Final Draft. Get your website. Get your business cards, and start marketing yourself. It will come.

I'm still in the middle of the game. I'm not at the top of my game yet. I will be. But it's been a rewarding experience—especially when you start getting some money and the applause. I don't feel you need to write every day, but you have to think about it every day. I think about scenarios every day.

Listen. Don't go to the airport and be plugged in. I don't have a smartphone. I like to see, listen to everything. Observe your surroundings. All the time, I'll hear something, I file it away, and it ends up in my plays.

*How do you remember all the stuff that you're picking up around you?*

**CD:** I just file it away in my head. Sometimes I do wish I had jotted it down. A lot of times stuff comes to me in the middle of the night. I do have to be better at jotting things down. When I was doing stand-up, I always had one of those little recorders with me. Always. You know, "Oh my god, funny man on the side of the road. Write a joke about it." I always did that. I should probably get one of those again.

But I do have a pretty good steel trap when it comes to remembering little witty one-liners. My friends and family don't mind when I "steal" lines or situations. They love hearing a little bit of themselves in my plays too. Now they will actually come to me with things. "This just happened to me—you should write about it in one of your plays." In *Couple Dating*, the characters are based on my husband and I. Obviously, my husband is not exactly like Bobby, but he is a mechanic. He owns his own shop. He is a dad who wants to hang with the old boys, his old crew. And Tess is ready to expand her limited friends and start hanging out with other couples. And that's very true. How many times do you want to hang out with another couple, and the wives love each other and the husbands, there's just nothing there?

We all have those stories in us, those funny stories that you remember, you tell at every party. Write it down. And maybe start out with a 10-minute play. Those are becoming very popular. They're quick, very satisfying. I can crank out a 10-minute play in no time. I was in something called the 24/SEVEN Theatre Project. It was out of Colorado, and they Skyped me in. Seven playwrights had seven hours to write a 10-minute play based on prompts we were given. We all had the same prompts. In seven hours, we had to turn over our plays. Then seven directors showed up. They cast it with 24 actors. So within 24 hours, they had two showings. That was cool. They told me. "You have to write two women, one man. You have to throw in this pop culture reference. One character has to be named this or at least reference this. You have to say this line," and it was a crazy line. It was about vegan muffins or something, and that was really cool. That was probably one of the cooler experiences I've ever had. Giving yourself a prompt like that and having yourself be forced to write—that'll get your creative juices flowing.

*That sounds really fun. Plus you've got the pressure.*

**CD:** I have to have pressure. It came easy to me because finally I was like, well, if I have to have this done—they're going to kill me if I don't. My play was *Kentucky Chickens*, a redneck comedy about two best friends who are auditioning for a TV singing competition called *Nashville Duets.*

It's a fun, rewarding gig to be a writer. Everyone wants to be a writer, right? Secretly, I wasn't comfortable saying I was a writer for a long time. You're like, when do you get to say you're a writer?

*I always get sad when people say that they're an aspiring writer, because there's a lot of hope there, but there's also so much fear.*

**CD:** Yeah. When you get to finally say you're a writer—wow. That's something amazing.

"Write about the scenarios in your
life that are funny. Write about
those memories that you have.
Write about your wacky siblings,
all your friends. Have fun, and
let it pour out."

— *Cricket Daniel*

# 6 Diane Raptosh

A graduate of the University of Michigan MFA Program, Diane Raptosh is currently the Idaho Writer-in-Residence. She was also the 2013 Boise Poet Laureate. Her most recent book of poems, *American Amnesiac* (Etruscan Press), was longlisted for the 2013 National Book Award. The recipient of three fellowships in literature from the Idaho Commission on the Arts, Diane holds the Eyck-Berringer Endowed Chair in English at The College of Idaho, where she teaches literature and creative writing, as well as directs the program in criminal justice/prison studies. *(Photo courtesy Eric Raptosh Photography)*

---

*I wanted to start out by congratulating you on your recognition as Boise Poet Laureate and Idaho Writer-in-Residence. What does it feel like to get that sort of recognition?*

**Diane Raptosh:** Boise instituted the Poet Laureate position in their sesquicentennial year for 2013 and they're currently taking a bit of a break now and trying to figure out a way forward. It was awarded through a competitive process. And I am the Idaho Writer Residence from 2013 to 2016, which is also awarded through the competitive process. So that is a $10,000 award of which we use, and during that period the writer goes around to different rural communities in Idaho giving readings.

*What made you decide to go through that application process?*

**DR:** It's a great way to raise awareness about poetry in the communities. So both of those opportunities gave me the chance to do that and that's pretty important. People often have ideas about poetry that do not jibe with the kinds of things poetry is doing today, or sometimes people had some traumatic experience with poetry way back when. I like to try to get poetry out there in such a way that it can renew or spur interest in poetry.

*Not everyone has really great teachers who, you know, teach them poetry and show them how it's evolved. You know, you just read through old ones and that's about it.*

**DR:** Exactly. And they don't realize that poetry does evolve as quickly as many other kinds of modes of writing, so they think all poetry still rhymes.

*What is it about poetry that keeps you writing?*

**DR:** I like the complexity that poetry affords. And you have to bring in the full panoply of what language has to offer with poetry—from the formal properties and the rhythms, to the connotations and the denotations.

Poetry is in a way a harmonizing of all the arts. It often feels like a language sculpture, a sculpture on the page. It feels like music. It feels like literature, which of course it is. It feels like dance. It's the best of all arts.

Of course, I'm not able to be objective about poetry. It just feels like the art that asks you to bring the most to bear. That's what makes it so hard to write—and what makes it so satisfying.

*Can you think of one poem that has been your favorite to write?*

**DR:** Right now, I'm writing book-length poems, so it's hard to say one particular poem. I guess the one I'm working on now. It's a very long poem.

*It keeps you coming back to it?*

**DR:** Yes. It does, and I hope that the next favorite one is the one after that.

*What got you into such a long form of poetry?*

**DR:** I started thinking in terms of really long poems, book-length poems—and this may surprise you—because I'm a really slow writer. If I have a concept I'm working on, it might free me up to work more efficiently and to think not just about this particular poem on the page. A whole series might evolve from a concept or a seed of an idea that I just keep nurturing. The longer form just suits the rhythms of my days, the incredible busyness of my life, because I can always have this concept growing in my mind. I can turn to it in short moments of attention or long moments of attention and keep growing it. Whereas if I'm working poem by poem, it's slower, it's more difficult, and it feels more artificial.

*That's really interesting. How do you keep your focus on that long form when you're working in those small chunks to make sure that you keep moving where you want to go?*

**DR:** Amazingly, life starts to imitate art. The process of that attention starts attracting information and phrases and language and new seeds that want to be brought into the work. And that awareness becomes a magnet for drawing in language, metaphors, concepts that want to be a part of the work. It's almost magic.

*Do you have any tools to capture those phrases that come to you while you're driving or at some other inopportune time?*

**DR:** That's a great question, and this is something I always ask my students to do: keep a journal. I have them keep a notebook-size journal. Then I show them the little tiny journals I keep, the little palm-sized journals. I always have one in my purse. I have one on both bed stands by my bed. I keep one in my car because I'm a commuter. And now that I have a smartphone, I also take notes on the little notepad as they come to me.

It just keeps me in a state of readiness. When a phrase enters the realm, I want to be there to capture it. The longer I write, the more it feels like writing becomes a state of receptivity, almost more than anything else, almost more than oh, what word am I going to plunk down next, but rather it's really an act of, again, staying in that state of readiness and being willing to be a kind of conduit.

*When you first start writing, you think "oh, you just make up a story and you write it down." But then your characters will surprise you, an event will surprise you. It'll be like, "I have no idea where that came from."*

**DR:** Exactly.

*And that's part of the fun.*

**DR:** That is the fun part because then it's like, "Wow, I'm not really writing this, I'm just here kind of taking dictation." The process isn't always that simple, but sometimes it feels that way.

*Another thing I thought was pretty interesting about you is that you teach both literature and criminal justice. That's not a combination I see a lot.*

**DR:** Almost 20 years ago, I had begun teaching a course called "The Prison Experience" with the sociologist at The College of Idaho, and I was aware of the large body of literature by inmates within the United States. It's a pretty rich tradition that's growing richer as we speak. My coteacher taught the sociology, and I taught the literature. We brought students into prisons and jails within the Treasure Valley. This became one of the most important classes in my whole teaching life because a poet always wants to think about freedom. Everybody in America hears the word freedom bandied about in ways that are alternately abused and truthful. So thinking about freedom is something that every poet likes to do.

Once it became clear how many people we're locking up—more than any country in the world, for longer terms and with a kind of capriciousness that seemed criminal—I decided I had to really give this a lot of my attention.

Eventually, the sociologist with whom I had been team-teaching retired, so I became the sort of sociologist slash writer in charge of the whole program. It's been one of the greatest opportunities in my teaching career, to bring these facts to people's attention. It has been such a well-kept secret in the United States.

Information's coming out now from a lot of scholars, thinkers, speakers, but when we first started teaching it, nobody had any idea what was going on and why. Today, my students are still quite shocked and hesitant to believe that the freest country in the world locks up more people than any other country.

*How do you think that your work in prisons has changed you as a writer?*

**DR:** I like to think about the metaphor of prison. Everyday life is about a negotiation of prisons—the various cages we must live in and free ourselves from just as a part of survival and regular existence. I like prisons and freedom as overarching concepts. Then going into these prisons and thinking about self and other, which is a major theme of any writer, makes one realize that there's, by and large, very little difference between me and other people who end up in prison. I've done many things that have landed other people in prison, and I was lucky. That breaks down this binary between us and them. I like to do that, to break that down for my students. I'll say, "Raise your hand if you've never broken the law." Nobody raises their hand.

That kind of awareness is good for cultivating compassion and understanding, a fuller knowledge of what it means to be human. Why do some of us end up in prison and others of us not? Usually, it's a matter of socioeconomic status, what kind of family you were born into—something we didn't get to choose. It encompasses a whole cluster of issues and questions that most writers are working with anyway, and working within the prison system, having that kind of exposure, has brought a lot of those issues into higher focus than might have happened otherwise.

*Have you taught any workshops to inmates?*

**DR:** I have. In fact, as Boise Poet Laureate, that's one of the things I did. Last summer, I taught a series of three weeks of three-hour writing workshops in the women's prison here in the area. That was a wonderful opportunity. They had a great time, and they were wonderful to work with. They gave a reading at the end of our time together, and they were able to invite anybody from the inside to attend. It was very well-attended, and they felt proud and empowered. But mostly, I felt lucky to be there and to have been a part of it.

*It's a situation a lot of people don't even think about putting themselves into and understanding.*

**DR:** It's true. And as Boise Poet Laureate, I wanted to give some workshops, and that was number one on my list. I don't think they expected that. Like, "Uh-oh, what have we gotten into with her?"

*Everyone needs the arts, no matter where they're living.*

**DR:** Exactly. And these people are part of our community, too. Most of them are going to get out and rejoin us and better that we're all working together helping to make our community stronger than to just ignore them.

*And positive connections with people who are not within the prison system is definitely a great thing. When someone gets out, if they know that there are people out there they've had positive experiences with, that can't hurt.*

**DR:** I think so.

*Have you always lived in Idaho?*

**DR:** Not always. I'm from Idaho originally. I did my undergraduate work at The College of Idaho, where I teach now, but I did my graduate work at the University of Michigan, and then I lived in Chicago for three years. I lived in Seattle for about a year. Laramie, Wyoming, for another year.

*What brought you back?*

**DR:** I was offered a one-year position at The College of Idaho and well, then the years started passing very quickly.

*What do you like about being in Idaho?*

**DR:** You know, I think Idaho is a very good place to cultivate an inner life, and that's probably what I like best about it, besides its people. I like the people of Idaho very much. They're very earnest and honest and decent and without airs. Maybe the overall quiet of Idaho, which is also sometimes its downside. You know, Idaho can be a little boring, but for a writer it's pretty good because it's quiet and there's a lot of space. The external space becomes internal space, and that's really beneficial for a writer.

*When you're feeling like you're lacking in inspiration, what do you do?*

**DR:** Panic. I try not to. I try not to fret too much about it. I read more, but I also try to let the fallow period be fallow.

But I'd be lying if I didn't say that I, you know, do start to panic and think, "Oh, my god. I'll never have an idea again. It's over." I can be pretty neurotic. We all can.

*But the more time you spend dwelling on it, the worse it gets.*

**DR:** For sure.

*Do you go out and hike anywhere or is there anywhere special that helps you connect?*

**DR:** I like the outdoors. I hike a lot. I live right near the foothills, and I do get outside a lot, no matter how my writing is going. I'm not positive there's a direct tie to being outside for me. I don't write a lot about the mountains and so on. I did when I was living away from Idaho, when I was missing all that, but now that I'm here, I don't address it directly in my writing. It probably has some kind of effect on me that I'm not aware of. Maybe it's just the space thing and the quiet and the languages of the wind and the natural sounds.

*That is interesting that you were writing about it when you weren't back in Idaho.*

**DR:** And now that I'm here, you know, it is the air that I breathe so I don't really have to write about it. I'm not necessarily a Western writer. I live here and I'm not sorry that I do, but my themes are no longer about the West. They were when I was much younger and, again, not living here and I was really missing it, but now those are not my themes.

*It must have been really great when you got that job offer so that you could come back.*

**DR:** I always feel a little bit like an alien wherever I'm living. For example, Idaho's very conservative politically, and my politics are not in keeping with those of Idaho. But there are many good reasons for living here and I feel quite lucky to live here.

*Do you think that little bit of not belonging helps you be inspired to write? Do you find yourself addressing those issues?*

**DR:** Just about every writer feels like an alien no matter where they live. And that feeling makes you study your surroundings and puzzle over them and wonder about them in a way that might not happen if you felt you really belonged. You might not have to wake up every day and say, you know, "Why are things this way and not another way?" And those are the questions that drive writers. My alien feeling is a good catalyst.

*Do you find that working with your students is another catalyst for you?*

**DR:** Absolutely. I love working with students because I love the exchange of ideas. I love being in a classroom. I don't always even feel like I'm the teacher in the classroom. I love to raise questions and jointly ponder possible scenarios with students on what they think are the most profound questions of the day. I like their freshness and their openness. I like working with students very much.

*I sometimes miss that college experience where you talk and you explore different ways of thinking and different ways of looking at the world and of solving your problems. That's just not something that you get a lot outside of that academic environment.*

**DR:** A classroom is a very convenient microcosm to be able to step into day after day to converse with your fellow human beings and see what they're thinking about and how they're coming to terms with the world as it is, which is changing so quickly. It's really a great honor to be able to do that. It's a luxury.

*Do you think that being in an academic environment also helps keep you inspired and moving forward in your writing?*

**DR:** Definitely, because I'm always reading a lot. I'd probably read a lot no matter what, but being able to ask the philosopher down the hallway a question or the theologian a question that's been swirling in my mind, it's a great luxury to have that access.

*And probably much more reliable and interesting than Google?*

**DR:** Google thinks itself to be all-knowing and all-powerful, but . . .

*It's only as good as the accuracy of what it can find.*

**DR:** This is true. Yes. Very true.

*Do you have any advice that you find yourself giving to your students a lot about their writing?*

**DR:** Keeping a journal, number one. And number two would be that receptivity. Just stay open, stay alert, stay awake and pay attention.

"Just about every writer feels like an alien no matter where they live. And that feeling makes you study your surroundings and puzzle over them and wonder about them in a way that might not happen if you felt you really belonged."

— *Diane Raptosh*

# 7 Greg Rucka

Greg Rucka began his writing career in earnest at the age of 10 by winning a county-wide short-story contest, and he hasn't let up since. He graduated from Vassar College with an A.B. in English and earned an M.F.A. from the University of Southern California's Master of Professional Writing program.

He is the author of nearly a dozen novels, six featuring bodyguard Atticus Kodiak, and two featuring Tara Chace, the protagonist of his Queen & Country series. Additionally, he has penned several short-stories, countless comics, and the occasional non-fiction essay. In comics, he has had the opportunity to write stories featuring some of the world's best-known characters—Superman, Batman, and Wonder Woman—as well as penning several creator-owned properties himself, such as *Whiteout* and *Queen & Country*, both published by Oni Press. His work has been optioned several times over, and his services are in high demand in a variety of creative fields as a story-doctor and creative consultant.

Greg resides in Portland, Oregon with his wife, author Jennifer Van Meter, and his two children. He thinks the biggest problem with the world is that people aren't paying enough attention. *(Photo courtesy Linnea Osterberg Photography, LLC)*

---

*One of the things that is interesting about what you do, is that it includes so much of a visual component, not just the written story. Does that affect how you look at a story?*

**Greg Rucka:** I've always considered myself a pretty visual writer. I tend to think very visually, which is odd because I suck at every visual art there is. I have no ability to draw or to sculpt. I can destroy just about the most simple model-making kit. But in comics, by definition, it's a visual medium, and the story needs to move visually. An ideal comic script is a script where if all the words were taken out, the story is still clear; where the dialogue or the text is secondary almost.

I tend to put a fair amount of thought to what I'm envisioning. But because I don't draw, I can't be married to it. The visual I imagine will be drawn and the visual that is actually drawn are very rarely the same. And one of the first things anybody who writes in comics has to learn is that you've got to get out of the way and let your artist tell the story. As long as the spirit is followed, I care very little about the letter. But that's for comics.

Prose is different because I'm controlling all of it. A comic book script is really a letter to the artist and everybody else involved. That script exists to say, this is the story we're telling in 20 to 24 pages, and these are the important elements of that story. But prose is a direct interaction with the mind of the reader. Consequently the crafting of prose is a very different thing than the crafting of a script. And in that sense, I tend to be very aware of my visuals because I tend to be very concerned with how I am describing. As I've gotten older and hopefully better at my craft, I have come to rely on the fact that there's a hell of a lot that the reader brings to the material on their own, and that if you can pick the right details and lay them out correctly, then the reader will do the rest of the work for you.

If you describe the room as, you know, old world stuffy and there was a dark brown leather overstuffed reading chair, then the rest of that space should be conjured. Whether there's an oriental rug on the floor; whether the books on the shelves in your mind's eye are leather bound; whether there are heavy curtains.

And especially in prose, because I spend a lot of time writing in first person, those details are also character details. If I have a character come in and say it was the kind of chair that you expect rich, fat people to sit in, that is as much about the character as it is about the room. Versus a character that comes in and says, you know, it was an 18th century overstuffed easy chair with brass fittings and a matching ottoman foot rest. One character is clearly passing a judgment. The other character is being far more objective.

*Has that type of thinking and writing come easily to you, or is it something that you had to really focus yourself on, getting more of that in your head as you're going along with a story?*

**GR:** I tend to work from character out, so that voice tends to be one of the first things that I know. And consequently, to know that voice is to know the person. To know the person is then to know what matters to them. So then I never really had a hard time reminding myself to be visual or to describe visuals. The problems I've always had have been, what's the best way to do it? And these days my prose has gotten so spare it's positively anorexic. And when I started, that was not the case. I would labor over making sure, you know, I used to have catalogues just so I could dress people, and use the proper terminology. And I reached a certain point where I determined that for me that didn't matter.

Elmore Leonard wrote this lovely little book that has his 10 rules of writing. In it, he talks about getting rid of the hoop dee doo, and as I got older I discovered there was a lot of hoop dee doo. I didn't need those details. Because very rarely is knowing exactly that they're called Capri pants, for instance, going to be relevant. The difference between taupe and tan, while a legitimate one, only matters to certain characters.

And one of the things I discovered early on is that unless you put something unexpected in the description of a character, especially of a main character, the reader has already decided what they look like. One cinematic example of this recently was where people were cranking over casting of *The Hunger Games*. "That character's not black." Actually, that character is black. It says in the prose, that character has dark brown skin. But some readers just didn't see him that way, simple as that.

The goal of any story is to keep you in it until it's over. I don't ever want to do anything that's going to eject you—especially in prose—from the narrator prematurely. You don't put a silencer on a revolver, and if you're in Eugene, you'd damn well better be certain which streets are one way and which ones aren't, because a reader is going to know. You can't head that way, you know?

*You mentioned earlier that you've had to let the artist do their job? Was that hard the first couple times?*

**GR:** Actually, it was never as hard for me because I've seen it be for some of my peers. I have some very, very dear friends who when they first started doing comics, I would literally watch them go panel by panel comparing it to what they'd written in the script. And then send back these copious notes, and I just, I couldn't do that myself. I tell almost every artist I work with this, "Out of 22 odd pages there's maybe one in there that I'm describing in a way that I would really like to try to see it executed." If you're working with the right people, they're going to bring the best game.

For instance, I'm doing *Lazarus* with Michael Lark, and I trust Michael absolutely. Any script I send him is subject to approval. He's got to be able to get in there and change what doesn't work, and oftentimes he does. The wonderful thing about Michael is that we're both so solicitous of each other now, that he'll say, "Oh, I was looking at this and I don't think . . ." And I'm like, "Just change it, man."

*So, what was it that got you into comics? Was it just that you loved comics and read them a lot, and that's what you wanted to do?*

**GR:** Well, you don't go into comics for any other reason than you love it. I started reading comics in first or second grade. I remember pestering my mom to buy me these little digest black and white reprints of the early Stan Lee/Jack Kirby comics. And I remember pestering and pestering and pestering her to get the Archie one or Incredible Hulk, or whatnot.

Then I got to high school and my peer group was reading *Uncanny X-Men* very actively. I wanted to fit in so I started reading it too, and that led to discovering there were other books in the store. In college, buying beer became more important than getting comics for a couple years. But I rediscovered them eventually.

I would go to San Diego Comic-Con back when that was a thing you could just decide to do, rather than spend three years saving to do. And I would pester editors. "Here are my novels. I would love to write a comic." And almost to a one they would say, "Get away kid. You bother me." But then I got lucky. I was introduced to the guys who were starting Oni Press and I pitched them *Whiteout*.

*Whiteout* is a really good example of why a work should be a comic. *Whiteout*, it's a visual story. It's such a visual story that it wouldn't work in prose. If a picture is worth a thousand words, it was going to take me ten thousand words to describe how fricking cold it gets in Antarctica. Or Steve Lieber can draw two panels and all of a sudden you want to put on a coat and get a fire going in the fire-place.

I've always loved the medium. I can never imagine myself as making basically my primary career in it, however. That still surprises me to this day.

*It is always funny how things work out.*

**GR:** I had stopped working in the mainstream for a while and I was trying to deal with any number of others things getting my life and my career sorted, and sort of my desires. I had a moment where I was talking actually to my agents—I have a literary agent and I have a Hollywood agent—and I found myself saying to them, "No, you guys don't understand. I need to be making a comic. If I'm not doing a comic, I'm not going to be happy." And that was sort of a surprising realization to me. I actually love the medium, despite all the brutality that I have been through in this industry.

*Do you think there is anything that is special about the Pacific Northwest that explains why there are so darn many writers here?*

**GR:** It's the climate. Somebody once said the reason there's really only one "great" higher-education institution on the West Coast (i.e., Stanford) is climate. You go to Cornell, Harvard, Yale, or Princeton, and for half the school year they're snowed in. They can't go outside and enjoy themselves, so they are at desks, in libraries, or in conversation with one another. And I do think there is something to that. I'm not sure I buy it 100 percent, but it is definitely part of it. Another reason there are so many people in the arts in the Pacific Northwest is that it's cheap. It's not as cheap as it used to be, but cost of living-wise it's still relatively cheap. And as a community forms, that community will grow because like seeks like.

There is something about the Pacific Northwest. Portland is such a hub of comics right now because there were a couple small publishers here, and more and more people moved here. And then there were more publishers. You can't throw a brick in Portland without knocking over half a dozen comics people. And I'm only exaggerating slightly. And now that the industry is sort of packing up and leaving New York in part because DC is moving to Burbank, leaving Marvel pretty much alone, I think that's only going to sort of continue.

*If you had three pieces of advice you could give to someone who wants to get into the industry, what would they be?*

**GR:** The first is work hard. You can only control one thing, and that is your commitment to your craft, all right? There's somebody out there who's going to put in ten thousand hours and write it and learn how to draw it, and if you put in five thousand hours, they're going to beat you. That's not to make it sound like a competition, but it is a question of your discipline and your commitment. That's number one. Those are the only things you can control.

Number two, to do anything, to do any work well you have to open yourself to other arts. You want to write comics, don't just read comics. Read novels. Read short stories. Go see plays. People who want to direct movies and only go see movies will never succeed as directors. You have to feed the machine. You have to understand all the things that are coming into play here.

And three, we live in an age right now where it is inexcusable to not promote yourself. We have the Internet, and there are forums all over the place. And if you write and you can't draw, there are ways to find artists. If you can get online, then you can publish online. There is no excuse, in this day and age if you really want it, to not be doing it. There just isn't. And if you don't put it out there, that's because you didn't want it enough. The way you do it is you do it.

I got very fortunate with *Whiteout*, but the fact of the matter is, *Whiteout* wouldn't have happened if I hadn't done everything required to get three novels published at that point, and a fourth on its way at that point. You know what I mean?

It just always comes down to commitment and discipline, because those are the things you can control, and that's the only thing. That really is, those are the only things you can control.

*When you look back at some of your earlier works, are there things you wish you could change?*

**GR:** Absolutely. I wouldn't believe any artist who says there aren't. That would require a level of arrogance I am not comfortable with. There are very few professions that demand constant improvement, right? If you are an accountant, right, then every year you have to master the tax code. But once you've got it, right, you have the rules. You've got your framework. But you write a story, you draw a story, the nature of what you're doing sort of demands that your effort next time is to be better. And it's always constant growth.

So of course, I look at stuff that I did 20, 25 years ago and I go, dear Lord. Sometimes I surprise myself and I'll read something that was pretty good. But more often than not I go, "Dear Lord. This is out there? How do I get it back?"

*If they would just invent that time machine they've been talking about all these years.*

**GR:** But then you get into trouble, right? There's a writer I know who's very fond of saying, "Don't let perfect be the enemy of good." I know it's an old quote, but it's a very apt one, especially for the arts.

There's a companion quote which is, "No story is finished, it's only abandoned." I could massage prose for years if I was indulged to do so, but nothing would ever come out. So you hunker down, and you live with it. And you hope the next thing is better.

"I tend to work from character out, so that voice tends to be one of the first things that I know. And consequently, to know that voice is to know the person. To know the person is then to know what matters to them."

— *Greg Rucka*

# 8 L. J. Sellers

L.J. Sellers writes the bestselling Detective Jackson mystery/thriller series—a two-time Readers Favorite Award winner—as well as the Agent Dallas series and provocative standalone thrillers. Her 16 novels have been highly praised by reviewers, and she's one of the highest-rated crime fiction authors on Amazon.

L.J. resides in Eugene, Oregon where many of her novels are set and is an award-winning journalist who earned the Grand Neal. She's also the founder of Housing Help, a charity dedicated to keeping families from becoming homeless. When not plotting murders or working with her foundation, she enjoys standup comedy, cycling, social networking, and attending mystery conferences. She's also been known to jump out of airplanes.

---

*I have been following you on twitter for a long time and enjoying your advice to writers and watching your career grow. It sounds like you finally made the transition to writing fiction full time now?*

**L. J. Sellers:** I did in late 2010. Right after I put all of my Detective Jackson books up on Kindle Direct Publishing, I did a really huge promotional phase and I started well. And at that time, I was freelancing. But I was able to quit my freelance business by the end of 2010. So now I'm a full-time novelist. It is great. I feel very privileged. It is an amazing thing, and I don't take it for granted.

*What was it like to make that transition?*

**LJS:** It was exciting. I woke up every day, just thrilled that I was able to connect with readers, that my books turned out to be popular, readers liked them, and I was getting good reviews. Sometimes I was pinching myself asking, was this real or can it last or are these sales going to continue or are they going to bottom out and I am going to be looking for work? So it was exciting, it was worrisome at times, but mostly it just felt like a tremendous culmination of 20 years of working my butt off to get there and then finally having it happen. So it was very exciting.

*How did you know you were ready to quit your other work?*

**LJS:** Because I was making enough money to pay my half of the bills, and I knew it was going to get better. I said it was going to get better. I looked at it from cost/benefit and decided the best thing I could do with my time is write more novels. It pays better than the freelancing, so financially it didn't make sense for me to be distracting myself with this other stuff. That was a very exciting moment, an exciting realization that actually writing stories was the most financially profitable thing that I could do.

*How were you able to manage it all those years that you were working full time and then juggling your freelance?*

**LJS:** Well, and raising three boys, too, so I was very busy. I wrote on the side. I wrote evenings and weekends. That was my pastime. I didn't do other things that I could have. I just kept doing it. Once I wrote my first novel, I was hooked. I became addicted to that process and I loved it. I am just not happy unless I am writing a story. So that kept me going and then I had some freelancing business going on the side as well, because I am industrious. I've got to do a little more, push a little harder here, so I just kept at it. I had a couple of setbacks, some low points where I said "Okay, I'm done. I am never going to write again!" That lasted about a week. Then I tried different things, I tried writing scripts for a while, because I got really burned out on spending years working on a novel and then having it not go anywhere. But eventually I came back to novels and it was a matter of perseverance, just getting up every day and saying okay, what can I do today to make this happen? Tenacity. It's about tenacity, it's about never giving up. I come from a long line of very stubborn people, but I found a way to make that work for me.

*Yeah. We stubborn people usually do find a way, because we are not going to give up until we do.*

**LJS:** That's right. And in the long run, I read articles by people who said, if you just hang in there, eventually your competition will either give up or die. So you will get where you are going. The other piece of great advice though, at some point, that I read was from a script writer who was asked, "Do you have any regrets to this, anything that you would do differently, what would it be?" And he said, "Well, if I had known that it was going to take 10 years to sell my first script, I would have found a better day job." And I took that to heart, because at the time I was waiting tables because it worked out better with my kids. But at that point I thought, "You know I've been at this a long time, and if I don't make a success of writing these novels, I need to have a job that feels good. That feels rewarding. That makes me feel good about myself as a human being. I need a better day job."

So that was the point where I said I was done waiting tables. It was time to go back to work in journalism. And it was a really good thing to do. In some ways, it took away some of my creative energies for writing, but at the same time I felt better about myself every day. So that was a good thing to do—to realize that I had to kind of function on two levels; that I had to believe thoroughly that I was going to make a success of my fiction career, but I also had to function in the everyday world as though it might not happen. I had to find another reality that was going to work for me and be just as rewarding. So make sure your day job makes you happy too.

*I like that. And was that at* The Register-Guard *in Eugene?*

**LJS:** *The Register-Guard* came later in my career. I worked for a pharmaceutical magazine for about seven years.

*At Advanstar?*

**LJS:** Yes. That was quite an education. I know more about pharmaceuticals than I ever thought I would.

*And you probably ever wanted to.*

**LJS:** It was interesting, though. I love medical information. I've always been fascinated by it, so it kind of gave me a good background for writing an occasional medical thriller, which I like to do.

*You also have mentioned that you worked with the police. How did you build that connection?*

**LJS:** It started with a phone call. The first officer I interviewed was in Salem, because I originally was going to set *The Sex Club*—the very first Jackson story—in Salem, because I wanted to involve the governor of the state. I just called there and said I am a novelist who needs background on this topic. They put me in touch with a detective who wanted to talk to me. I interviewed him and it went very well. Once you've made that first connection and they decide they trust you or like you, they will put in a good word for you with the next person you want to interview.

When I went to talk to the Eugene Police Department, I said, "I interviewed so and so in Salem." And then you talk to the first person there and then they open the door for you to talk to the medical examiner. I've been to the crime scene lab and they gave me a tour there and I've talked to a FBI agent and all kinds of people. So once you open that first door and they decide that you are trustworthy and you tell them, "I am not going to make the police look bad" or "If you're going to tell me things that are background information, they will not be quoted." And you just build trust and then you make the connection. And I always take free books to give them. That always helps.

*Were there any other ways that your day job in journalism has helped you?*

**LJS:** Journalism teaches you to be a very self-disciplined writer, so I don't have writers block. I don't have days where I can't produce anything because as a journalist you don't have that luxury. You have to get up, you have to go to work, and you have to write. Copy's due, so you write. I don't worry about the lede. I don't worry about the first sentence. I just start. I can go back and fix it later. Journalism taught me that you just start writing. You can always clean up later, but you have to produce the words. There is no staring at the screen and waiting for inspiration. That has been a boon to me to be able to just make myself write and know that it will all come out in the long run.

*Do you think that the editorial process also helped you to kind of understand that the first words that come out don't have to be perfect?*

**LJS:** Exactly. In journalism—especially in magazines—it is a process, the reading and the content editing and the copy editing and then the proofreading. It helped me understand that is how my novels had to be produced. When I self-published, I applied that same standard of editorial quality to my novels that we did to the magazines or the newspapers.

*A lot of times writers who haven't been in that world get scared when they get edits.*

**LJS:** Or upset. That is the other thing about being a journalist: it teaches you not to be attached to every word that you write, because ultimately you're writing for someone else. You learn to have a little bit of objectivity and to step back from your writing. Not every word is perfect, and it's going to get changed — and that's okay. As long as the content and basic story I'm telling comes across the way I want it to, that's what matters. You learn to accept the fact that you're going to be edited and you're going to face some criticism. You have to learn to process it and know that it's making you better at what you do. Sometimes it doesn't feel like it. I admit that.

*Do you have any advice for someone who might need a way to get that feeling of objectivity about edits without going into journalism?*

**LJS:** Find a really good editor to work with. Find someone that you like and trust and who knows the genre you write in. And hire someone who is going to be constructively critical instead of blunt. Start with somebody who is going to be diplomatic and coach you in your writing. There are a lot of great editors out there. It is just a matter finding the one that is going to work for you.

Then be open to what they have to say. If you are doubtful, give it to someone else and say, "My editor wants me to do this. What do you think?" It is okay to seek feedback from other professionals as well. That's the other thing is you have to network and establish relationships with other authors who are willing to share their successes with you and steer you in the right direction.

*Do you feel like there is something special about the Northwest that keeps you writing and keeps you creative?*

**LJS:** That's a good question. I think indirectly in the sense that I am very happy living here. I think it is a very rewarding place to live. It is also very secure, especially lately in the world where there is some crazy weather happening. We just don't deal with that here, so there isn't that constant disruption. My lifestyle tends to be very predictable and very calm and very satisfying. And that helps me as a writer.

And there is a certain aesthetic to the northwest that is good for the soul, which is good for the writing. I feel lucky to be here.

*And that joy and happiness and just ease of life has to really make it easier to be creative. Do you have a goal for your word count every day?*

**LJS:** I do when I am writing the first draft of the story. I have a goal of 2,500 words a day. I don't always meet it, but I have that goal, and I work really hard to get there. I have an Excel sheet where I keep track of my daily word count. I have to record it. I have to look at it. I am accountable for those words, so if I have a low day, I know how much I have to make up for the next day to stay on track.

After the first draft is done, I stop worrying about word count. The second draft is clean up, but my goal is to get that first draft down as quickly as possible, because I have learned that is how the story goes best for me.

*About how long does that end up being? What is a good amount of time?*

**LJS:** About two months. The fastest I have ever done a first draft was about six weeks. That was *Deadly Bonds*. That story just came together so well. I have also spent as long as five months writing a first draft, which is not good.

*How about the rest of it? The second draft. The editing process.*

**LJS:** That depends whether I am sending my work to Thomas and Mercer, which publishes my Jackson series, or whether I am self-publishing, which I do with my Dallas Series. Essentially, the second draft takes anywhere between two and four weeks. At that point, I print it out and I give it the first major print edit, which is very different for me than online. I catch so much more when I read it on paper. It is a very tedious process, but I do that.

Then I send it to beta readers, and I may have to wait up to two or three weeks for everyone to get me their comments. I do another draft. Then it goes to an editor. The editor typically takes two to three weeks. Then I do another major print edit.

That's when I self-publish. When it's with Thomas and Mercer, I send it off to them after it comes back from the beta readers. They take the editing process from there. And that takes longer because they are on a different production schedule. And then they go through a content editor and then a copy editor and then proof readers. They send me the work after every one of those people read it and have their comments. And that process typically takes a couple of months to go through with them as well.

It takes about five to six months depending to get a book into its final, I'm done with this, mode.

*Are you able to work on more than one first draft at a time?*

**LJS:** No. I tried that. I may have an idea in my head already for my next book that I may be taking notes and maybe doing a little outlining, but typically no. I've never written two stories in first draft at the same time. I am a multitasker, but not when it comes to producing a novel. My novels are complex. I can't imagine trying to keep two timelines straight at the same time. Two character casts to worry about, no. And there is no reason for me to do that. I am not under contract with publishers, I am not writing for anyone else's deadlines but my own, so there's no reason to try to do that.

*Without those external deadlines, what keeps you on track?*

**LJS:** I am just a very self-motivated person. You might say driven, obsessed. But I get up every day with the idea that I am going to get as much done as I can because that is what feels good to me. I set up my production schedules and I meet my goals, because that is how I live my life.

*I love that you both self-publish and traditional publish. And it does sound like the traditional publishing model has influenced a lot of what you do on the front end of your self-published books, so they don't have a lot of the errors that have turned a lot of people off.*

**LJS:** Exactly, but that comes from my background working on magazines and newspapers. Even though we call it traditional publishing because I am with Thomas and Mercer, I really don't think of them as a traditional publisher. They are a publisher, but they're not a New York publisher. They are not one of the big five, and they do things very, very differently than traditional publishing. So I never had a New York publisher, and I am glad for that now. There were times in my life when it was a source of great anxiety to me. I thought I needed a New York publisher, and I came very, very close at times. But Amazon has this same process in which they are very thorough about content and editing.

*It is amazing how easy some people think self-publishing is, because a lot of the mechanics of it are easy. You have a file, and you can upload it.*

**LJS:** It's so much more complicated than that. It is a business. When you decide to write and publish a novel, you are basically starting a business. And you have to approach it that way. You have to look at it from a business perspective. You have to think about what you are going to invest and how. And you have to plan what you can expect for a return on your investment. There's a lot to think about in terms of marketing.

I studied the industry for about a year before I jumped in and started self-publishing. So I felt like I had a pretty good idea of what was going on, how I needed to approach it, what I needed to do. I had lists and lists and lists of people to contact, marketing strategies to try, processes, I set up production schedules. I really studied the business before I jumped in. And I invested heavily, too. At the time I had been laid off the journalism job. I was freelancing, and I had no backup. But I invested in good cover design and editing, et cetera. I treated it like a business that needed a substantial investment.

*Where did you go to study it? Did you read books about the industry? Did you talk to people? Did you take classes?*

**LJS:** Most of it was online in terms of reading blogs, watching what other people were doing, reading some books that were available at the time. One of the main people that I followed and modeled my strategy after was Joe Konrath. I looked at what he was doing. At the time, he was writing a police procedural series and self-publishing it, and he was successful. I said if he can do it, I can do it. And he has been very helpful to a lot of writers. He has put a lot of information out there.

*If you could go back and do it differently, do you think that you would have done it the same way?*

**LJS:** I think so. I can't really look back at anything I did that felt wrong. There was money I spent on marketing and promotional that didn't pay off. If I could have that money back, that would be nice. But it is a learning process and not everything you do in terms of marketing is going to work. The only thing I do regret is spending money on public relations campaigns, because they just don't pay off. And there are a couple of print ads that I paid for that I don't think paid off at all. But other than that, I have no major regrets.

*What has been your best bang for the buck marketing thing?*

**LJS:** Some of the newsletters over the years have been really helpful. Back when I first started, *Kindle Nation Daily* was a really great way to get your book in front of readers for not a lot of money. That's the one that really helped launch my books and get them selling so that I got that algorithm support. I've also used *Fresh Fiction*. They have a pretty good list in terms of a newsletter. *BookBub* is a really good one for getting your book in front of a lot of readers. They are getting a little expensive. The prices keep going up, because they know they have the corner on that promotional market now, but they have done some good things for me.

*How did you find these different places?*

**LJS:** *Kindle Nation Daily* is run by Steven Windwalker, one of the early Kindle adopters. He basically made it his goal to know everything about Kindles and to share information with this group of readers that signed up for his newsletters. I learned about him from following people's blogs and watching what other writers were doing. Sometimes these newsletters will reach out to authors as they're trying to grow their business. So it's just a matter being plugged in online to right connections and right sources.

And I have a lot of author friends, and they would email me and say, "What have you done that's worked lately?" And I would tell them what I tried. Or I would email them and say, "Hey, you got anything new that I haven't tried?" And they'd say, "Oh yeah. I just found this great Fussy Librarian Newsletter" or something else new. So we help each other out.

*Can you think of anything else that you would want to tell your fellow writers?*

**LJS:** You have to be patient, because it doesn't happen overnight. And you're much more likely to be successful if you have more pieces written. It might even be a good idea to not to put your first book up there the minute you've got it done, especially if you're writing a series. Write a couple of books in the series first, and release them a couple months apart so that you build a series and the readership quickly that way. If you've got one book and you put it out there as a single book, it may not sell well. And if it takes you a year or a year-and-a-half to write another book, you can be very discouraged during that time by the lack of sales and lack of response to your single titles. So in some ways it might even be easier to get a couple of books done, and then get two or three books out there in a very short order at the same time, because you will build momentum faster.

I had kind of a weird process in that I was self-published, then I had a small publisher, then I was self-published again. When I self-published again and made a success of it, I uploaded five books in a very short timeframe. So I had a lot of books all at once. The first time I self-published, you had to buy 3,000 print copies and it was very expensive. And so I had a long and interesting process in trying to get my books out there. I've tried everything, as they say. But it's worked out in the long run. It all paid off.

*And that's how you learn.*

**LJS:** That's how you get where you are going. You make a decision that you are going to make it happen, and you don't give up. And have your work professionally evaluated. Send your work to a content editor, a story doctor, or even agents. It's important to have feedback about whether your work is commercially viable. Once you have that feedback, go ahead and invest your money. But if you are not getting that feedback, then you need to go back to the basics and take some more workshops, make sure your work is in fact a marketable product before you spend your money.

"There is a certain aesthetic to the Northwest that is good for the soul, which is good for the writing. I feel lucky to be here."

— *L.J. Sellers*

# 9 Suzanne Williams

Suzanne Williams is the award-winning author of 50 plus books for children—from picture books and easy readers to chapter books and middle-grade fiction series. A former elementary school librarian, she lives near Seattle. Her picture book *Library Lil* (illustrated by Steven Kellogg) won the New Mexico children's choice award in 2000 and was on several other state award lists. She is co-author (with Joan Holub) of the popular *Goddess Girls* series (for ages 8–12), *Heroes in Training* (ages 6–11), and *Grimmtastic Girls* (ages 8–12). Other series include *Fairy Blossoms* and *Princess Power.*

---

*You grew up in the Northwest, and you talk on your author site about how much you have always loved reading. I'm wondering if you think there's something particular about the Northwest that made you want to read a lot?*

**Suzanne Williams:** Probably all those dark, cloudy days. All that rain. Because there's nothing cozier than sitting in a nice chair curled up with a good book. I would suspect that weather does have an effect. Don't they say that in Seattle, people read more books per capita than pretty much anywhere else in the country?

*There's nothing like a book on a rainy day.*

**SW:** My mother taught first grade forever in Eugene, and she was always bringing books home. And she took me and my siblings to the public library at least once a week. There are four kids in my family. My parents sparked a reading habit in all of us.

*Do you think it was mainly that they brought books home to you and were like, "Oh my gosh, this is so exciting, you have to look at this," or that they modeled the reading behavior?*

**SW:** I suspect the modeling was a big factor. But I can still remember how enjoyable it was to be sitting beside my mother on the couch with my siblings all around and her reading to us. The book that I remember her reading the most was *Winnie the Pooh*.

*You say on your website that you really didn't think of yourself as being a writer, but even back in elementary school your teachers talked about your creative writing abilities. When do you think you started making stories?*

**SW:** At least by third or fourth grade. But I didn't have any basis for comparison, so I just assumed that everybody did this. You know how you are when you're a kid, you just assume that everybody's life is pretty much like your own? You don't overthink it. I didn't realize until much much later when my mother had found one of those student booklets of writing that teachers put together that my story was actually much longer and more detailed than some of the other stories. My stories showed that I read a lot. I was almost always more interested in reading than writing. I enjoyed writing, but it wasn't anything I ever considered doing for a career.

*So what made that shift happen, when you did decide to write?*

**SW:** It was being a children's librarian, working at an elementary school and reading all of the different books I was putting on the shelves. I started thinking writing for whildren would be fun and something I'd enjoy trying. I actually had those thoughts in the back of my mind in my early 20s, but I didn't really know how to go about doing it. Once in a while I'd take a stab at writing a story and then think, "Oh this is so crazy. What am I trying to prove? I'm no writer." So I'd put the story away. What I ended up doing is getting a journal. That was what I used to satisfy my urge to write for many years.

My mother-in-law's death finally got me to move from thinking about writing to actually taking steps to do it. She had cancer in her early 60s and it metastasized and spread really fast. It was about a year and a half after she was diagnosed that she died. Her death brought it home to me that we really don't know how much time we have on this earth.

If there's something you want to do, you can't just keep thinking, "Someday I'll do this." I needed to take some steps to reach my goal. Just reading books about writing for children hadn't done it for me in the past, so I decided I needed to take a class. A formal class of some kind to help me get started because I didn't have a journalism or creative writing degree. I took a children's writing course from the Institute of Children's Literature. It was a correspondence class, although it's offered online.

It was mostly short story writing for children's magazines. If I had to do it all over again I'd ask for a particular instructor instead of just having one assigned to me. The person who was assigned to me was a good instructor, but his expertise was non-fiction. Because I was more interested in writing fiction, I would have read the biographies of the instructors and then requested that I be matched with someone who wrote the kind of thing I was interested in writing.

One valuable thing the class did was give information on how to go about sending things out to try to get published. Of course, that's changed too. A lot of publishers now take email submissions.

You don't send stories by snail mail anymore.

*And it helps having so much information available on the Internet. It's easier for people to understand the process, because the process scares a lot of people away.*

**SW:** When I have talked to groups of children's writers, I stress breaking that whole process down into small bites. Make one goal for yourself, for example, to go online and read a particular article about the process of getting published. Because if you look at that huge overall goal of writing a book and getting it published—that's just overwhelming. You have to start with something small and concrete.

My concrete step was taking a writing class. And at the end of that class, I actually had to send something out, which happily got published. It was an article for an education magazine, and it was non-fiction. It wasn't the kind of thing I ultimately wanted to write, but it was a start.

*It's great that they made you go through the process actually rather than just reading about it.*

**SW:** Right. By the way, for people who might not have the money to take a class, because some of those can be expensive, there are a lot of free classes online these days. Or you can connect with other people who are also trying to get published and form online or face-to face critique groups—there are so many more options than there used to be.

*Do you think there's anything particular to children's publishing that you want to give people advice about?*

**SW:** It is a genre of its own, so it does have different rules than other types of writing. For example, the child characters should solve their own problems. You don't have an adult step in at the end and make things right. That's one rule I learned early on.

*That would make me really mad if I were a kid reading the book.*

**SW:** Exactly. And you don't want to talk down to children in children's books. Kids are a lot more sophisticated than some adults give them credit for being.

Also, you don't have to end a book so that everything is fine and dandy, but you should end it with some kind of hope? No really really bleak endings, especially for younger children.

*You don't want to send them into a tailspin of depression.*

**SW:** For sure, and depending on, again, the age of the kids, you may want to go a little lighter on the description and heavier on the action and dialogue to keep their interest.

*One of the things that is really interesting about children's books is just the level of collaboration on the different parts of the story, because there's both the writing and the visual.*

**SW:** If it's a picture book. Many novices think that if you write a picture book, you've got to find somebody to illustrate it. But that's not how it works. You write the story, and your publisher handles the illustrations. When you're writing, you might make suggestions if an illustration should show something different than what's in the text, especially if some kind of joke is involved. I sometimes put in parenthesis that the illustration might show such and such happening. I always couch suggestions for illustrations in terms of "might show," because I don't want to trample on an illustrator's feet. They often have better ideas for what will work.

With the first book or two, you might not see any sketches as your book is being illustrated. For my very first book, which was a picture book, I didn't see the illustrations until the book was actually published. With books that came after that, I was shown more and more and got a chance to look at sketches early on and make a few comments. But I am careful only to make comments on things that don't match the text. I am not going to tell an illustrator how to do his or her work. I'm not qualified to do that!

*Did you find that it was a little bit scary, especially on that first book?*

**SW:** A little, I guess. The book was called *Mommy Doesn't Know My Name*. It's a mother-daughter story about a little girl who is confused when her mother calls her all kinds of pet names (like chickadee, pumpkin, and monkey) instead of her own name. Anyway, I was picturing realistic illustrations in my head when I wrote the story, but the actual illustrations were very abstract. The main character had a big head on top of a tiny little body. But the pictures grew on me. I was still a librarian then, and reading the book aloud to groups of children, I realized that the kids really did like the humor in the illustrations.

*Sometimes putting that out there and letting someone else illustrate it and bring it to visual life seems like a good exercise in giving up some control.*

**SW:** That's definitely true. And it did help that I was a librarian because I was used to seeing a range of illustration styles. So it was easier to give up that control. And also the fact that I was not an artist myself—I wouldn't presume to tell an illustrator how to do their work.

*Do you get to work directly with your illustrators now?*

**SW:** Usually you don't work directly with them, and you're not emailing back and forth either. All communication is done through your editor and through the art director at the publisher. So the editor would send me sketches and I would comment back to her. Then she'd share comments with the art department, and they would talk to the illustrator. So it's all kind of third person.

Most everything I'm doing now is targeted toward middle grades, so illustrations are mainly book covers and a few interiors. My co-author, Joan Holub, and I don't usually work directly with our cover artists, but we will see black and white sketchs of covers before they are colored. Truth is, we're now getting covers before we've written the books. Our editor will come to us and say, "Oh I need some cover ideas on such-and-such book" that we haven't even started to write yet.

*Wow. You guys really are on a timetable.*

**SW:** We'll scramble around and think, "What could go on the cover?" We send our ideas, and the cover artist will put together a cover sketch for us to review. We'll make recommendations if we need to. Something like, "Can you age the character up a little bit? She looks like she's about 10-years old, and she needs to be more like 12 or 13." Or "Can you change the clothes because they look too modern?"

*That coauthor relationship was another thing I wanted to talk to you about. How did you guys get together?*

**SW:** Joan and I knew each other through the Society of Children's Book Writers and Illustrators, SCBWI, a professional organization.

The regional group has conferences in Seattle once a year, so I met her at one of these conferences while she was still living in Seattle. We just hit it off, and two or three times a year we'd get together and go out to dinner. We'd have these long two or three hour gab fests about what we were working on and the writing business in general. After several years, she said, "Have you ever thought about writing with a partner, writing with somebody else?"

I hadn't, so she asked if I'd consider it. At that point, she and I had both written series. I think I was writing my fourth or fifth series, and she had just written a six-book series for Scholastic. And she said "You know, by the time you get to that fifth or sixth book, you're just going 'Ah, I want to be done with this!' I wouldn't mind writing another series, if I didn't have to be responsible for every single book in the series." So we decided to give it a shot.

Next time we got together, we both came with a couple of series ideas. We decided on *Goddess Girls*, one of Joan's ideas. And we just divided up the work of putting together a series proposal. Because we both had published quite a bit by then, we didn't have to produce a complete first draft of a book to convince a publisher to take a chance on our idea. Having each done several series before, we could get by with a one-page synopsis for each intended book and an overall summary of the theme, the various characters, that kind of thing. And a draft of maybe three chapters of the first book.

We each picked two goddesses that we wanted to be among our main characters. Joan's were Athena and Artemis, and I picked Persephone and Aphrodite. Then we came up with story lines. Two and a half years later—it took that long—our agent sold the series to Simon and Schuster. By that time, Joan and her husband had pulled up stakes and moved to North Carolina.

*Oh wow.*

**SW:** She lives in Raleigh, so by the time we started writing the books together we were living states apart. Of course with the Internet, it's not hard to collaborate with somebody that's far away. So our partnership has all been done at a distance, and I've seen Joan once in the six years or so that we've been writing together. It's all phone calls and emails.

*So how does it actually work being a co-author? Do you write one of the books and then she looks at it, and then she writes the next book and you look at it?*

**SW:** That's pretty much our process. We know some co-authors who write every other chapter, and we thought that sounded really ambitious. Of course, our process has evolved, the longer we've been working together and the tighter the deadlines get.

We started out writing one series together. Then we added another series and another. Now we're trying to scale back. Before we even start an outline for a book, we have a phone call where we brain-storm ideas for that book. That's really helpful because sometimes you'll write an outline for a book and then your partner looks at it and says "I don't think these ideas for the first chapters are working at all." So we head that off by having a conversation beforehand. Then, after that discussion, the person who is writing the first draft will create an outline. The other co-author looks at it and makes suggestions and changes. Then if it's my book to draft, I'll write the first draft and send it to Joan and she does draft number two.

At the beginning I would get back all of her revisions—we track changes in Microsoft Word—and I'd see this sea of red lines, and think, "Didn't she like any of it?"

But now I hardly give that a sea of red lines a second thought before I click on the box to accept all changes. I get on with writing a third draft. Occasionally, there will be a few logic problems when working this way. That's the main thing that happens with a partner. They may change one thing and not realize that it didn't get changed all the way through. So you'll have to be on the lookout for that. But even if it was just you writing a story, you'd still have to be on the lookout for logic problems and other inconsistencies that creep into a story

One hard thing about writing a series is keeping track of what's happened in the past. We used to try to keep a document that would have all of that stuff in it, but we never had the time to update it. So now we mostly use the find feature in previous PDFs of books to try whatever details we need. Not terribly efficient.

*Whatever works.*

**SW:** So we trade every other draft. Then after a story goes to the editor and she sends back notes, we both do a revision, but whoever wrote the first draft will go through the story first, and then go to the partner for a few more changes. back to the first partner who will then accept the changes. Whoever did the first draft will then also be the first one to look at the copy edit. We used to both look at everything, but last year, we decided that only one of us would look at the galleys.

*Do you think the fact that you had a relationship beforehand really helped you build trust faster than you would have with a stranger?*

**SW:** Yes, I'm sure that's true. The reason we ended up partnering is because we knew from our long association and talks that we had similar work habits, writing styles, senses of humor, and liked writing for the same age groups. The last thing you want, by the way, is to partner with someone who you feel is not going to pull their own weight. We knew we could depend on each other to do a fair share of the work, and that's crucial in a partnership.

*That relationship is one people don't really understand.*

**SW:** Yes, it's almost like a marriage! By the time one of our books gets published, it's a definite collaboration and we've both made lots and lots of changes to each other's initial first drafts, hopefully for the better.

*What are the differences between writing some of your earlier books that were not on contract, and writing these that are on contract? Other than the time frame, what feels different to you?*

**SW:** When you're writing under a contract, you have deadlines, and that can be a good and a bad thing. It requires you to really plan out what you're going to do, draft chapters one and two this week, for example, and three and four next week. I'll write out exactly what I need to get done each week in order to make that deadline.

But writing under deadline is not bad either. I've gotten spoiled these last few years because I haven't had to go out and try to sell anything. All of the books I'm writing are already sold.

If I had to choose one or the other, yes, I definitely prefer working on contract. I know I'll see my work in print. Going back to writing on spec would be hard. It's pretty sweet to know the book you're writing is actually going to see daylight.

"If there's something you want to do, you can't just keep thinking, 'Someday I'll do this.'"

— *Suzanne Williams*

# 10 Eric Witchey

Eric M. Witchey is an American writer living in Salem, Oregon. His short fiction has appeared in numerous print and online anthologies and magazines, such as *Polyphony, The Best New Writing 2012, Low Port, Short Story America, Realms of Fantasy, Space Squid, Fortean Bureau, Thug Lit, ClarkesWorld, Jim Baen's Universe*, and *Writers of the Future.*

He has won recognition and awards from New Century Writers, Writer's Digest, Writers of the Future, Ralan.com's Clincher Contest, Ralan.com's Grabber Contest, The Ralph Williams Memorial Award, and the Eric Hoffer Prose Award Program. His how-to articles have appeared in *The Writer* and *Writer's Digest* magazines. He has taught seminars at many conferences, including on the Greek island of Crete (Write in Crete, 2005) and near Lake Chapala in Mexico (The Lake Chapala Writer's Conference, 2012).

---

*I wanted to talk a little about your background. I know you're not from Oregon, but you've been here a while. What was it about the Pacific Northwest that brought you here and what keeps you here?*

**Eric Witchey:** I had a choice to go to New Jersey or Oregon when I got out of graduate school. I'm a fan of the outdoors, hiking, skiing, rollerblading, bicycling, et cetera, and Oregon offered more opportunity for that. When I moved here, I was on the path to being a writer, but I didn't know that Oregon was the writing community that it is. Once I got here, it was really wonderful to discover that there's this amazing writing community between San Francisco and Seattle, basically. The West Coast writers, there are more of them really than anywhere else in the country, and I found them to be very welcoming. I've worked with many organizations out there, and there's just nothing like it in the rest of the country.

*Yeah. I know. I didn't really realize that until I got hooked up with Willamette Writers. I mean you know there are writers from Oregon and from other parts of the northwest, but I never realized the density.*

**EW:** More writers per capita than anywhere else in the country, possibly the world. But there are not more writers per square mile. There are more writers per square mile in New York. What you have to figure is that the entire population of Oregon is half the population of New York City. I tell people you come to the Willamette Valley, you can't swing a dead cat without hitting a writer. And there are good things and bad things about that. The good thing is you have this wealth of information, and generally speaking it's shared. And the bad thing is you have this wealth of writers, which means that you often are selling to people who are already writers. What I say to people is selling books to writers is like selling ice to Eskimos, but often you find yourself in the position that you're selling your writing to writers, and that's kind of silly really.

*But, hey, we appreciate good writing, so we tend to buy a lot of it.*

**EW:** That's true. We often see writers at book signings. I went to a signing the other day for a friend of mine. There were about 15 people there, and five of them were writers. It's kind of quite fascinating.

*That makes it a really great place for you to be teaching writing, though.*

**EW:** That was pretty much accidental. I didn't set out to teach writing. I set out to learn to write.

I had background in linguistics, and I found it very difficult to learn from existing writers. I would ask specific questions about how to do something, and they would give me very vague and general answers. Something like, "This needs to have more energy," or "There aren't enough beats here." And then I would ask, "Well, what is a beat?" and they couldn't give me a definition. That just didn't mean anything to me in terms of executing manipulation of text.

So, I fell back on my linguistic training. I started analyzing structurally the manipulation of the actual characters on the page and the various responses that created. I started analyzing text that existed before, other peoples' writing, and I started seeking out writers who could answer my questions specifically. And that led to actually meeting a guy named James N. Frey. He introduced me to things that were more useful to me as a structural analyst—to come to the text and say, "If you change the text this way, you'll get this response from the reader."

Once I went down this path, it became no longer acceptable for me just to achieve a result. I had to achieve the result and understand how I achieved it. And my test for that was that I only understand it if I can teach you to do it and you succeed. And that became how I tested myself to see if I knew something.

I would identify a technique. I would articulate it. Then I would articulate the textual manipulation that results in what you want. And I would turn that into a document, a little module. I would take that and give it to somebody and say, "Does this make sense? And can you do this?" If they could, then I had succeeded in understanding the concept. At the same time I was doing that, of course,

I was practicing lots and lots and lots, writing lots of fiction.

The end result of that was people started seeking me out to teach. They started seeing those papers and saying, "Will you teach this to us?" Pretty soon I was teaching at the Pacific Northwest Writers Association. People would see me there and they'd invite me to travel and teach. Then I was teaching at Willamette Writers and the Oregon Writers Colony. Private students started seeking me out. Editors for *The Writer* and *Writer's Digest* asked me to write articles for them.

*How do you fit writing in around all that teaching?*

**EW:** That's a funny question to me. You do it in the morning before you do anything else. If you talk to a professional writer, they're going to tell you that they have time carved out. It's very rare that I meet a writer who writes based on inspiration. The more appropriate question is what time of day do you write? And they'll tell you from 7–12 or from 4:00 in the morning until 6:00 when the kids wake up—they all have different answers, but they'll all have very specific answers.

For me it's 8:00 till noon every day. If I don't write, then it's a miserable day. Didn't used to be that way. That's a habit that developed. It's like runners who run every day, you know, their adrenalin comes up. In fact, I have a bell, and I've trained myself to hit flow states when I ring the bell. So, I start my sessions by ringing the bell and then I do a practice session. I get up in the morning and I sit down and I roll my dice, and I get three three-digit numbers. And then I go to a list of things that I have accumulated over the years and find those three numbers. I end up with randomly selected topics, story prompts. And then I have a technique that I'm practicing every day. I do that for 15 minutes. I write as fast as I can, attempting to execute that technique while hitting those three randomly produced topics. Sometimes I get short stories out of that and sometimes I don't, but that's not the goal. The goal is to execute at speed a particular skill so that when I'm doing composition, I'm doing composition through that filter. I'm literally causing my brain to adapt to that level of fluency and technique so that when I'm writing very quickly I can express stories through the filters that I've overlaid by that type of adaptation. Did that make sense?

*It did. That's really interesting.*

**EW:** I find it fascinating. And again, linguistic training combined with practice and desperation brought me to these things. There are writers who write really, really fast. They produce material at unbelievable rates. So, I asked them how they do it. I took the various stories they told me and synthesized them to find what they had in common. This is what they think they're doing, but what was it that all these people have in common that is useful?

Carol Emshwiller was one of my teachers, and I asked her one day, "Carol, do you do outlines for your books?"

"Oh no. I never do outlines. I just never do outlines. I just put my characters on the page and they know what to do. And I'm always surprised by what they're going to do." Then, she stopped dead and looked straight at me and said, "But you should."

I asked why, and she said, "I used to do outlines. I did hundreds and hundreds of outlines and then one day I didn't have to."

And that clicked for me. This is the pattern for natural language acquisition and fluency. That's how it works. Story is an extension of natural language, and if you practice the patterns of story you

become fluent. You no longer have to think about how you're producing story. You just produce it, and that mapped on to all of the
experiences I had gathered from other writers.

So, I started looking at those other writers and asking, "How did
you get here? What was the process?" And there was this very
standardized process of development they went through to get
to the point where they were fluent in story. Many writers are at
various stages in that development, and they have different techniques. And every story is a different puzzle, so you apply different
techniques, but generally speaking the ones that were producing at
speed and producing a high quality of material had become fluent.
They weren't thinking as much about story as they were thinking
about character and then expressing through the structures of story.

*That's really interesting, and it does make sense because you always hear
the most prolific writers say, "Oh no. I just go in there, and I just write."*

**EW:** Yes, but they did not start that way.

*Then everyone tries to do that, and they're like, "I'm never going to finish
this novel. I've been working on it for 25 years now."*

**EW:** Right. And that's one of the errors people engage in. They
revise the same book over and over so they're not learning new
techniques. Well, they do learn new techniques, but they don't learn
the deeper, underlying structural techniques because that's already
set. So, they have systemic error in the story that they never really
quite address. They have to put that aside and do a new story in
order to progress as writers. And that's another common characteristic. The writers who are fluent, they have written many, many
stories instead of rewriting one story for many years.

Another of my teachers, Steve Perry, I was talking to him one day and I told him that I'd had something like 17 revisions on a short story, which I ultimately did sell. But he laughed at me. I asked, "What's so funny?"

"Eric, if you haven't got it right by the third revision, throw it away and do a new one. It's faster."

At that time, that wasn't true for me because I hadn't internalized the story the way he had. Fast-forward another five or six years, and it is true for me. It's much faster to write a new story than to fix this broken one.
Bottom line for me, in any individual story I do not know which techniques I will be using, but I know that there are techniques in my toolbox. So it's a puzzle. What will make this story function?

I get in trouble because I write across genres. I get told fairly frequently that I have to pick a genre, but the assumption is that I have to pick a genre in order to build a client base, in order to build a following, in order to be a *New York Times* best-selling author, or whatever. I consider that just patently absurd. I would have to share that value system, and I'm not capable of it. I need to understand the puzzle. It's an obsession. When I look at each story, I'm looking at what will make that story the best story it can be. Sometimes that means it's going to be science fiction and sometimes it means it's going to be fantasy, and sometimes it's erotica and sometimes it's romance, and sometimes it's mainstream or literary.

The question is, who's the audience and what are the techniques you're going to use? For example, technical writing is a different audience, different purpose, different set of techniques, but you need all of those techniques. I still have to think about whether I'm dealing in independent clauses or fragments. I still have to look at it and say is this going to be better as a compound complex sentence or do I need to have a subordinate opening clause? Do I need to minimize the subject of the sentence or maximize it, or do I want passive voice or active voice?

All of these things are things I think about when I'm doing tech writing, but you think about them for different reasons than you do when you're doing fiction. In technical writing, I'm going to probably use present tense, active voice. And now, I'm writing a piece of fiction, and I want to hide a clue; so, suddenly, I'm going to shift to passive voice in order to hide the agent. And I'm going to use an embedded serial list in order to hide a clue, which I would never do in technical writing.

*I'm so glad you brought up your technical writing. I'm always interested to hear how someone successfully navigates doing both fiction and commercial writing, because so many writers think one robs from the other.*

**EW:** Writing is writing. Audience and purpose determines the form. I've done ghost writing. I wrote an article on male participation and the modification of a woman's body during pregnancy in order to reduce the pain of a birth. I ghost-wrote this article for a men's magazine on behalf of a female midwife who travels the Third World teaching these techniques. I ghost-wrote a cookbook on how to use potatoes as a nutrient-rich part of your diet. I have written many, many technical documents for high-tech industry and Q&A documents on how to do job interviews, both how to do the interviewing and how to be the interviewee. I established the audience and purpose, and then I established a form for that audience for that purpose.

Shift over to fiction, and the shift is not all that great. The difference is instead of giving you a set of instructions or a set of objectives, data points that will be useful to you to solve a problem, I am now shifting to the delivery of a set of subjective perspectives through a series of experiences that will allow you to avoid problems. That's what fiction does. It lets you vicariously experience other people engaged in horrible circumstances and coming up with their solutions so that you can reduce the risk in your world. That's the function of fiction since we were teaching each other how to use pointy sticks to not die killing mammoths. That's where stories come from. Let's sit around the fire. How did it go today? Well, Bob died. He didn't have a pointy stick. How do you make a pointy stick? Well, let me tell you. Now we're telling stories. Same thing.

So what's the shift? The shift is from objective to subjective. What's the shift in language? This audience needs second-person instruction. Okay. Over here, I have subjective experience through a third person narrator that occasionally melts into character. So, I'm moving from external to internal. I'm moving from objective to subjective depending on whether I'm a narrative voice or character voice. It's still the manipulation of little black squiggles on a white background. In one case I'm saying, "Here, consciously reevaluate this data and use it to solve your problem," and on the other side I'm saying, "I will manipulate the little black squiggles to guide you on a dream, basically take you on a dream walk." It's still writing, it's just different purpose, different audience, slightly different mechanisms. One case you're using the writing to engage objective cognitive activity and the other case you're using the writing to engage in essentially the manipulation of a dream state. Opposite ends of the spectrum. Same tools.

*How do you read now that you have studied and worked so much on the structure?*

EW: Do you know Isaac Asimov's quote, "The worst thing I ever did to my reading was learn to write"?

It's actually easier for me to listen to a story than it is for me to read one. If a storyteller is really competent, not just as a storyteller, but also as a line-by-line mechanic, a technician, I can immerse myself in story. And writers that do that for me are people like most of the magical realists if the translations are good. Sometimes in Spanish. Christopher Moore. Some of my more favorite genre writers, Terry Pratchett. I can get lost in Terry Pratchett partly because he's always got his tongue so firmly in his cheek that I cut him a lot of slack. It's just fun.

Mainstream novelists I often have difficulty with because the language is quite often not designed to keep me in the illusion. The language is designed to allow me to be aware of the language. And I like that for different reasons. So I read that material for different reasons.

It definitely adds a level of difficulty to just enjoying a story, particularly if I'm reading it on the page. I love my e-reader. I find that it is easier for me to read, to digest the story on an e-reader than it is on the page. I don't know that this is true, this is speculation, but my e-reader is sufficiently different from the printed page that it doesn't kick in my beta activity, my cognitive activity in the same way. My editor doesn't just jump up.

I can pick up something that is intentionally bad and immerse myself in it without any trouble because my editor turns off because I know it's supposed to be bad. I can pick up something that's really, really good and immerse myself in it. It's the stuff in the middle that makes me crazy.

*What do you want other writers to know about your process?*

**EW:** There is a spectrum of process. On one side you have purely intuitive writers who succeed. On the other side you have purely cognitive writers who succeed. Every writer is somewhere on that spectrum, generally speaking. They have a position in that spectrum. Their position changes as they mature. My position tended toward the cognitive and has moved toward the intuitive as I've matured as a writer. Other writers go the other way. Every story has a mix of positions on that spectrum. Some stories come out purely intuitively. Some stories come out purely cognitively. Some stories are mixes.

The idea that any writer can teach you to write is a fallacy. Writers can teach you how they write. Writers can show you tips and tricks. Writers can show you processes and patterns of success and patterns of failure. But only the individual can teach themselves to write by making that material available and by practicing with it until they break it. If I want writers to understand anything it is that you do not understand technique until you have taken it to its absolute limits and internalized it and broken it. When you see how it can be used to fail, to work functionally, and then take it to a point where it no longer functions, that's when you're learning.

Writers who play it safe when they write, fail. Writers who constantly test the boundaries or are constantly testing the relationships of techniques or constantly testing patterns, those are the writers who succeed.

I get accused of being an analytic, cognitive writer, and nothing could be further from the truth. I have used analytic cognitive tools in order to develop isolated techniques that I can practice so that I am a more intuitive writer, if that makes sense. I often don't think about story structure at all when I'm writing. I am too busy writing. But I have spent many, many thousands of hours internalizing those patterns so that I don't have to think about them, and it's important for writers to know that, especially in the electronic publishing age.

Anybody can publish a book. And everybody does. And there is a profound reduction in attendance in conferences, in writing conferences because people don't think they need to go to learn. They often don't think there's even a market rebound where people reject the idea of agents and editors. It's sad and absurd because what they're doing is embracing mediocrity. They're not testing themselves against a standard of excellence that is very important in their development, and I think that's a sad thing to see.

I published some e-books through IFD Publishing, and I have only published material they have asked me to do or material that I believe in that has not sold elsewhere. So I have a story called "The Apple Sniper." It's a short story that I really like. Okay, well, so I put it out through IFD. I asked them, 'Can I put this out?' And they're like, 'Yeah, sure.' But even then it went through a professional editor and proofreading, and then it went out, and I still found flaws in it.

*Oh yeah. You always do.*

**EW:** Exactly. My position is to advocate endless, ceaseless experimentation—a quote from Baron von Richthofen. They asked him how he became such a great flyer, and he said endless, ceaseless, restless experimentation. That's it. That's the thing.

What else do I want writers to know? Every story that goes out does good in the world whether you know about it or not. Somebody needs the message that you've sent. Stories are often messages in a bottle. They go out. People read them but you may never know. And I firmly believe that every message that you put out in that bottle somebody needs it and that's why you put it out. If you had the passion to write the story and it goes out and gets into print, somebody out there needed to read it. And I've had enough validation of that, I have enough stories out that occasionally I'll run into someone and find out that it had an effect in their life.

Let's see. What else? Don't stop. Man, I think every writer you talk to is going to tell you that. The thing that aspiring writers need to know is there is only one death, and that's the death of stopping. It'll eat you alive. Even if you go through endless dead times where you're having trouble, if you continue, there'll be a moment where you have the new revelation that you need.

"It's very rare that I meet a writer who writes based on inspiration. The more appropriate question is, what time of day do you write?"

— *Eric Witchey*

# Conclusion

So what did we learn from all of these conversations?

There is a lot of good advice in the old truisms, such as don't give up, read a lot, and write a lot. After decades of trying, L.J. Sellers kept at it and became successful enough to quit her other employment. Suzanne Williams came to writing after a lifelong love of reading. And Eric Witchey has spent his career practicing technique, whether it results in a saleable story or not.

Our writers also pointed out the importance of learning, whether it is through formal courses, conferences, or critique groups.

But there was some other advice that really hit me—and really cut across the conversations.

## Get uncomfortable

There is something to be said for pushing past your boundaries and going places you'd never go, and not just in your writing. Mary Andonian and Diane Raptosh have volunteered and taught in prisons, and they both saw a profound effect on their writing.

Raptosh uses her experiences visiting prisons as fodder for her work exploring concepts of freedom. And Andonian has taken what she learned about the inmates in the prison where she volunteered to inform her current project, a screenplay that has taken her far out of her writing comfort zone, just like her initial visits to the women's prison took her out of her physical comfort zone.

Of course, you don't have to go all the way to prison. You can take a vacation in a location you've never been to. Or you can explore a genre you aren't familiar with, as Andonian also did when she transitioned from novels to screenplays. She'd been published as a novelist, so there was a certain level of comfort inherent in continuing in novels. But once she tried screenplays, she found they were her true love.

This also happened to Cricket Daniel. A former stand-up comedian with a near-constant desire to be on stage, she found her true calling when she began writing plays and moving off the stage to let others bring her words to life.

## Screw the muse

Inspiration is a wonderful thing. But it's fickle. And it doesn't pay the bills.

Sometimes it hits during your work day, when you least need it. Sage Cohen captures those fleeting thoughts so she can revisit them later during her personal writing time. She uses paper to capture thoughts.

Inspiration also strikes when you're out living your life. Raptosh has a series of notebooks that follow her through life, from a palm-sized one that can fit in her purse to the voice memo feature on her smartphone for times when writing is inconvenient. Who hasn't been hit with the muse while driving? There is even a set of water-resistant notepads on suction cups so you can write down ideas that come to you in the shower—none of the writers I spoke with mentioned using them, but they can be a great tool if that's where the muse likes to visit you.

Sellers learned to just write from her magazine and newspaper experience. When you're working on a daily paper or a monthly magazine, you simply don't have time to wait to feel like writing. It has to happen. So she doesn't struggle with writer's block or wait for the muse to visit. She simply sits down and gets the work done. There are some writers who don't think commercial writing is worthwhile, but deadline-driven writing definitely teaches a level of discipline.

And in our discussion of finding time to write, Witchey said he's never heard of a professional writer who was able to sit and wait to be inspired. He has found a way to put himself into the writing mode so that he can achieve his daily writing goals—and get his daily writing fix.

## Find your flow

Witchey has a system he uses to get into a flow state—the state where writing comes naturally and without significant struggle. He has created this process over the years, training himself through repetition and writing practice to get his mind and body into that state in a short amount of time. Without a ritual, it may take 20 minutes or longer to get into flow—or flow may never come that day.

Think about your writing rituals. Do you brew a cup of tea? Sit in the same spot and turn off all unnecessary computer programs? Or even pull out a notebook to write in longhand? Have you tried anything different to get your mind into the writing mode? What has worked, and what hasn't? See how you can force yourself into the right mental state to write and begin doing that each time you write. The only advice I have is to avoid using something like Salt and Black Pepper Kettle Chips. Your waistline will thank you.

## Be in business

Writing—whether you write novels, nonfiction, short stories, poems, or screenplays—is a business. As an author, you'll need to market your work to editors, publishers, producers, and, ultimately, readers or viewers. You'll want to make sure you're able to hit your financial benchmarks, so that as Sellers did, you can pay your part of the monthly bills.

When Sellers was looking at self-publishing her work, she spent much of her time exploring the business side of selling books, and she learned enough to become a full-time novelist. Witchey and

Cohen both use commercial writing projects to ensure that they reach their financial goals. When you become a writer who views your career as more than a hobby, you'll need to make a budget to see how much you need to earn. You'll need to study marketing and public relations so you can get your writing the attention it deserves. You'll want to learn the steps of the publishing process so that you provide a high-quality product to your readers—or decide to partner with a publisher to help with some of the process.

## Define your own success

Patricia Briggs has hit a goal many of us define as a success: she's a multiple *New York Times*–bestselling author. But she hasn't reached the levels of fame that some of her compatriots in urban fantasy have hit. And she's perfectly happy to be where she is. For her, success isn't being the most well-known author. It is being able to make enough money that she can write the books she wants to write on the timeline that works for her.

Witchey sees himself as successful when he is able to understand and use a literary technique. For Daniel, success is getting produced and seeing her plays brought to life on stage, although a regular gig writing for television wouldn't hurt.

The key here is finding your own measures of success and following a path that will help you achieve them. If the New York Times bestseller list is your goal, find out how people get there and see how those processes will work for you. If it is something else, explore what it will take to get there—and be clear with those around you what you're working toward.

## Collaborate and network

Many of the writers here found great power and pleasure from working with others. Williams found a great partnership with a like-minded writer that has allowed her to explore a more reasonable approach to series writing that splits work up and provides a constant source of inspiration and help. And she recommends networking with other writers to get feedback and support.

J. Anderson Coats keeps connected with a tribe of writers at the same point in their careers who provide each other advice and support as they navigate publishing. She has also connected with her readers through social media to help her stay authentic and speak to her young adult audience.

Daniel loves the process of collaborating with her producer and her actors to make her plays the best they can be—often making changes based on what they see on the stage and how the audience reacts.

And Greg Rucka and Suzanne Williams have the most fully collaborative writing jobs. When Rucka writes a script for a comic book, he trusts his illustrator and allows that artist to take control of the story and make it their own. And Williams says she trusts her co-author so much she doesn't even review the changes she sends—she just accepts them, trusting completely that the changes are right. Their willingness to give up control is inspiring, especially for those of us who have some control issues about our writing.

Work to find a group of writers that can keep your creativity flowing, offer advice, and help you work though writing problems and issues. We are lucky in the northwest that as Witchey says, you can't swing a dead cat without hitting a writer. Use the nearby writing organizations such as Willamette Writers and the Pacific Northwest Writers Association to connect.

But most of all, keep writing. This is the most critical element all of the writers interviewed for this book mentioned. The more words you put on the page, the better you'll be at it. Whether you want to see it as a musician practicing scales, like Sage Cohen does, or becoming fluent in story, as Eric Witchey approaches it, it will be the most important thing you do.

"See how you can force yourself
into the right mental state to write
and begin doing that each time you
write. The only advice I have is to
avoid using something like
Salt and Black Pepper Kettle Chips.
Your waistline will thank you."

— *Jennifer Roland*

www.gladeyepress.com

*Books (and calendars) for the Northwest reader.*

CELEBRATING THE

PACIFIC NORTHWEST